11/12

# MANHATTAN LSAT

# Reading Comprehension

D1475425

## LSAT Strategy Guide

This guide shows you how to adjust your reading approach based on the nature of the LSAT and the types of reading skills that it is assessing. Learn to read with purpose and to understand of how the LSAT constructs tempting wrong answers.

Reading Comprehension LSAT Strategy Guide, 3rd Edition

10-digit International Standard Book Number: 1-935707-86-8
13-digit International Standard Book Number: 978-1-935707-86-8
eISBN: 978-1-937707-28-6

Layout Design: Dan McNaney and Cathy Huang
Cover Design: Evyn Williams and Dan McNaney
Cover Photography: Alli Ugosoli

# INSTRUCTIONAL GUIDE SERIES

---

### Logic Games
(ISBN: 978-1-935707-84-4)

### Logical Reasoning
(ISBN: 978-1-935707-85-1)

### Reading Comprehension
(ISBN: 978-1-935707-86-8)

# PRACTICE BOOKS

---

**10 Real LSATs Grouped by Question Type**
**Practice Book I**

(ISBN: 978-1-937707-36-1)

**15 Real, Recent LSATs**
**Practice Book II**

(ISBN: 978-1-937707-12-5)

MANHATTAN
LSAT

October 23, 2012

Dear Students,

In your hands is the end result of years of hard work. At the core of this book is the brainpower of the most talented teachers and curriculum developers that I know. Many moons ago, Mike Kim and Dan Gonzalez pored through years of LSATs to figure out what makes the test tick and together they wrote our original Logic Games Strategy Guide. One found mastering the LSAT to be nearly effortless while the other had to work hard to unlock the LSAT's inner logic and tendencies; it is the combination of the two that underlies our curriculum.

We pride ourselves on teaching that goes far beyond lecture-style classes. This means not only that our students are actively engaged in the material, but also that our teachers are always rethinking how to unlock complex ideas in ways that make students truly understand. Each new edition of this book incorporates what we've learned from helping our students learn. So, along with thanking our teachers and book team for their invaluable input—especially Brian Birdwell, Dmitry Farber, Cathy Huang, Elizabeth Krisher, Dan McNaney, Matt Sherman and Patrick Tyrrell—I must thank our students for raising their hands to ask and answer interesting questions.

At Manhattan LSAT, we're always looking to improve and to provide you with the best prep available. While we hope that you'll find the book you're holding to be exactly what you need, we appreciate any feedback you may have, whether it's positive or not. Please e-mail me at noah@manhattanlsat.com with any comments, and we'll be sure to consider them for future editions.

Good luck as you prepare for the LSAT!

Sincerely,

Noah Teitelbaum
Executive Director of Academics
Manhattan Prep

# HOW TO ACCESS YOUR ONLINE STUDY CENTER

# If you...

> **are a registered Manhattan LSAT student**

and have received this book as part of your course materials, you have AUTOMATIC access to ALL of our online resources. To access these resources, follow the instructions in the Welcome Guide provided to you at the start of your program.

Do NOT follow the instructions below.

> **purchased this book from the Manhattan LSAT Online store or at one of our Centers**

1. Go to: http://www.manhattanlsat.com/studentcenter.cfm.

2. Log in using the username and password used when your account was set up. Your one year of online access begins on the day that you purchase the book from the Manhattan LSAT online store or at one of our centers.

> **purchased this book at a retail location**

1. Create an account with Manhattan LSAT at the website https://www.manhattanlsat.com/createaccount.cfm.

2. Go to: http://www.manhattanlsat.com/access.cfm.

3. Follow the instructions on the screen.

Your one year of online access begins on the day that you register your book at the above URL.

You only need to register your product ONCE at the above URL. To use your online resources any time AFTER you have completed the registration process, login to the following URL: http://www.manhattanlsat.com/studentcenter.cfm.

Please note that online access is non-transferable. This means that only NEW and UNREGISTERED copies of the book will grant you online access. Previously used books will not provide any online resources.

> **purchased an eBook version of this book**

1. Create an account with Manhattan LSAT at the website https://www.manhattanlsat.com/createaccount.cfm.

2. Email a copy of your purchase receipt to books@manhattanlsat.com to activate your resources. Please be sure to use the same email address to create an account that you used to purchase the eBook.

For any technical issues, email books@manhattanlsat.com or call 800-576-4628.

# TABLE *of* CONTENTS

# Chapter 1 of Reading Comprehension

# Reading Comprehension Overview

# Why Study Reading Comprehension?

**1**

***I already know what Reading Comprehension is. What can this book do for me?***
Reading comprehension is a staple of almost all standardized testing. You saw it on state tests in elementary school, you saw it on the SAT, and, of course, you will see it on the LSAT.

There is a reason for this: reading comprehension exams are a great way to test an individual's ability to absorb, comprehend, process, and relate written information in a time-efficient manner. These are skills you'll need as a lawyer, by the way.

It seems to make sense, but is it really possible to accurately quantify a person's level of reading comprehension? Can't we all, by looking at our own lives and experiences, see that our own level of reading comprehension is something that *fluctuates* from situation to situation?

Let's look at a few scenarios:

1. Ted is an electrical engineer. He has been working in a niche industry for years, but it's very easy for him to understand and evaluate articles on engineering concepts that fall outside of his specialty, even when he isn't familiar with the specific terminology involved. He's recently become interested in the stock market, and has been trying to read up on it. However, he's having a lot of trouble understanding and organizing the investment advice that he's read in various financial publications.

2. Sally is a freshman in high school. She has mastered the art of instant messaging, and sends and receives hundreds of messages a day. She filters them and organizes them easily, and is able to weave together a cohesive understanding of the lives of her friends. However, when she tries to organize the personalities and events of 18th-century Europe from her history textbook, she's hopelessly lost.

3. Jane is an English literature professor, and a luddite. She's finally getting around to using the internet to communicate with her students. She is surprised by the short, abrupt, and casual messages they send to her. She is unable to catch subtlety and has difficulty interpreting the tone of the messages she receives. She tries to write short responses back, but invariably ends up sending emails that are too long and take her too much time to put together.

It's easy to see how different types of Reading Comprehension exams would score Ted, Sally, and Jane very differently. The truth is, none of us has a definable (or quantifiable) level of reading comprehension. Put simply, our reading comprehension ability is highly variable. It depends on many factors, including our familiarity with the subject matter, the manner in which the material is written, the purpose of our read, and our overall interest and focus level.

For a few of you, the strengths you possess as readers already align with the LSAT Reading Comprehension test. In other words, your ability to read and comprehend LSAT passages is similar to Sally's ability to organize and synthesize her text messages. However, for most of us, the complex passages that appear on the LSAT do not naturally fall into our reading "sweet spot." So what do we do? We must work to become intimately familiar with the characteristics of LSAT passages, and then define our reading approach based on these characteristics. In other words, we must expand our sweet spot to *include* the LSAT.

This book is designed to lead you through this process, one step at a time. If you are not already an "LSAT reader," you will become one by the time we are through.

**MANHATTAN**
LSAT

1

# Your Path to Success

Mastering Reading Comprehension on the LSAT is not easy. It takes a lot of work to get to the point where you can read and understand an LSAT passage just as comfortably (or at least *almost* as comfortably) as you would the articles in your favorite magazine. Here are the steps we're going to take to get you there:

**1. Build familiarity.** In general, when readers read material that they already know something about, they tend to comprehend at a much higher level than when reading something about an unfamiliar topic. Ted, from the previous page, is a perfect example. Material related to engineering, even if out of his direct area of expertise, is easier for him to read and comprehend because he has a framework of prior knowledge upon which he can "hang" any new, related material, and he understands the fundamental logic of engineering principles. When he reads about the stock market and investment theory, however, he lacks a preexisting framework of knowledge and he struggles to comprehend.

In an ideal world, we would all be experts on the subject matter covered in LSAT Reading Comprehension passages, and we'd be able to leverage our prior knowledge to better understand what we read. Ted would ace the Reading Comprehension section of the LSAT if every passage were related to engineering!

The issue is that, for the purposes of the LSAT, we cannot rely on prior knowledge of the subject matter to help us. For most of us, the good majority of passages will cover subjects that we know little about. Should we spend our preparation time anticipating and studying everything that could appear in an LSAT passage? Not very practical, and because of the broad net of possibilities, not to our advantage.

We need to generate a different kind of framework off of which to "hang" new information. Instead of using a *subject matter* framework, we will use a ***structure*** framework.

Consider the following example:

> Knock, knock.
>
> Who's there?
>
> Shelby.
>
> Shelby who?
>
> Shelby coming round the mountain when she comes.

Imagine for a second that you'd never before in your life heard a knock-knock joke. This text would make absolutely no sense to you at all! Only because you are completely familiar with the form of knock-knock jokes are you able to immediately process and understand the joke. You know, for instance, that lines 1, 3, and 5 are spoken by the joker, and that lines 2 and 4 are spoken by the person to whom the joke is being delivered. You know to expect a play on the name "Shelby" in the punchline. You know that the joke will likely not make a whole lot of logical sense, but you're able to read it, understand it, and appreciate it nonetheless because you related the *structure* of this particular text to previous experience with knock-knock jokes.

1

LSAT passages are built around a very consistent structure as well. If you learn to see this structure, it will be much easier for you to organize the various elements of the passage, and to understand their significance.

**2. Define your reading perspective.** The perspective from which you read can have a huge impact on how you make sense of a given piece of text. Let's go back to high school for a minute. Imagine your English teacher has assigned Shakespeare's Hamlet, and that your reading of the play will be evaluated in one of the following three ways:

1. You will be given a quote exam, during which you will be asked to identify certain lines taken from the text of the play.
2. You will be asked to write an essay about the major themes in the play.
3. You will be assigned one of the roles in a high school production of the play.

If you were asked to complete a quote exam, you would read with a particular focus on learning the characters and understanding the basic plot. If you were asked to write an essay on the major themes, you would interpret and extrapolate, attempting to uncover the author's implicit messages. If you were asked to act out the play, you would read with an eye towards character development, and you would pay close attention to the emotions of the characters at different points in the story. Needless to say, your interaction with the text, and your interpretation of the play, would be greatly affected by the perspective that you adopt.

We'll spend a good deal of time in this book defining an advantageous perspective from which you'll want to read all LSAT passages: from the perspective of a law student. This perspective will help you quickly recognize and organize the most important information in a given passage.

**3. Understand the core competencies.** Every Reading Comprehension question on the LSAT tests your ability to do one or more of the following: (1) IDENTIFY a piece of supporting text, (2) INFER from a piece of text, and (3) SYNTHESIZE multiple pieces of text in order to make a general interpretation.

We'll spend a chapter examining the characteristics of these core competencies. You'll develop a keen sense for what correct answers should accomplish.

**4. Identify patterns in incorrect answer choices.** Success on reading comprehension questions depends, in large part, on your ability to eliminate incorrect answers. For the hardest problems, the right answer can be unpredictable and not ideal. In fact, it is often easier to spot wrong answers than it is to spot the right answer. With this in mind, it is important that you develop a sense for how the testwriter creates incorrect choices.

We'll examine the common characteristics of incorrect answers and learn to use our understanding of these characteristics to effectively eliminate bad choices.

With these four tools in hand, you'll be ready to master Reading Comprehension on the LSAT. Before we get started with the process of expanding your reading "sweet spot" to include LSAT passages, let's discuss some of the logistics of the Reading Comprehension section of the test.

MANHATTAN
LSAT

# Reading Comprehension on the LSAT

1

## Section Breakdown

The entire LSAT exam is comprised of the following sections (not necessarily in this order):

| SECTION | QUESTIONS | SCORED? | TIME |
|---|---|---|---|
| Logic Games | 22–23 | yes | 35 minutes |
| Reading Comprehension | 26–28 | yes | 35 minutes |
| Logical Reasoning (1) | 24–26 | yes | 35 minutes |
| Logical Reasoning (2) | 24–26 | yes | 35 minutes |
| EXPERIMENTAL | 22–28 | no | 35 minutes |
| Essay | 1 essay | no | 35 minutes |

Note that every LSAT exam will contain one Reading Comprehension section that will count towards your final score. Thus, just about one-quarter of the total questions on the LSAT will be Reading Comprehension questions.

Keep in mind that the Experimental section could end up being a Reading Comprehension section as well. If you do receive two RC sections on your exam, only one of those two sections will actually count towards your final score (unfortunately, it's impossible to know which one).

## Scoring

Each Reading Comprehension question, and every other question on the LSAT for that matter, is worth exactly 1 point. If you answer a question correctly, you will be credited with 1 point for that question. If you answer the question incorrectly, or if you fail to answer the question, you will be credited with 0 points for that question.

It is important to note that there is no guessing penalty on the LSAT. An incorrect answer is scored the same as a "no answer." Thus, it is to your advantage to answer every single question on the exam, even if some of those answers are guesses.

During the scoring of your exam, your points are totaled and then converted to a scaled score between 120 and 180. The conversion depends on the performance of all the other test-takers who took the same exam; a standardized curve is used to assign your scaled score.

**1**

## Subject Matter: Do I have to know about the law?

Every Reading Comprehension section contains four passages. You can expect to see one passage per section in each of the following four subject areas:

| Subject Area | Expect to see passages on... |
|---|---|
| THE LAW | legal history, international law, legal theory, social ramifications of law |
| NATURAL SCIENCES | evolution, biology, chemistry, physics |
| SOCIAL SCIENCES | history, political science, sociology, economics |
| HUMANITIES | literature, art, film |

The LSAT does NOT expect that you have any prior knowledge when it comes to the law, natural sciences, social sciences, or humanities. All the information you will need to answer the questions will be contained in the passage. That said, students with a certain level of familiarity in these subject areas will have a slight advantage. As we discussed earlier, the more familiar you are with the subject matter, the more likely you are to comprehend what you are reading.

## Pacing

You will have a total of 35 minutes to complete the four passages. This works out to 8:45 per passage. However, you will need to be faster than 8:45 on easier passages in order to have the extra time necessary for the more difficult passages. Generally speaking, the four passages on the LSAT are arranged from easier to harder (easier passages at the start of the section and harder passages at the end; this is a tendency, NOT an absolute). With that in mind, consider the following pacing plan for a Reading Comprehension section:

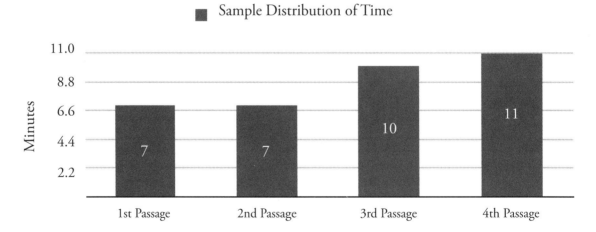

For each specific passage, time must be allocated to reading the text and answering the questions. In general, it is recommended that you spend more time on answering the questions than on reading the text, but this ratio of time spent will depend on your own personal style and your particular strengths and weaknesses.

1

As you go forward in this book, and as you practice more on real exams, keep returning to the following list in order to hone your process:

| SIGNS THAT YOU ARE SPENDING TOO LITTLE TIME IN THE READING PROCESS | SIGNS THAT YOU ARE SPENDING TOO MUCH TIME IN THE READING PROCESS |
|---|---|
| You have trouble recognizing the central argument. | You try to memorize and notate every single detail in the text. |
| You have trouble organizing the information in the passage relative to the argument. | While you are reading, you try to go beyond understanding the text relative to the central argument and try to see what else you can infer. |
| You don't understand the role each paragraph plays relative to the rest of the passage. | |
| You have trouble paraphrasing the purpose of a paragraph. | You spend a lot of extra time trying to understand specific elements of the text, elements that ultimately don't show up in the questions. |
| You don't have a clear sense of the author's opinion. | |
| You don't have a clear sense of which opinions contrast one another. | You feel rushed while going through the questions. |
| You often miss problems pertaining to the passage as a whole. | You often feel that you do not have time to go through the process of elimination. |
| You often have to go back and reread the text in order to answer questions about the passage as a whole. | You often answer off of a "gut" feeling. |
| You do poorly on questions that ask you to compare the text to some sort of analogy. | You often feel that you do not have enough time to return to the text to verify answers. |
| You often feel lost when you have to go back into the text to find answers to questions that ask about a specific detail. | |

Again, remember that there are no absolutes when it comes to timing. Use this book and your own practice to get a sense for how you should allocate time between reading the text and answering the questions.

Let's get to work.

MANHATTAN
LSAT

# Chapter 2 of

## Reading Comprehension
### Part 1: Read Like a Law Student

# Recognizing the Argument

# Getting Familiar

Read the following passage in two to three minutes. Underline and notate however you would like. At the end of your reading process, look over the text again, and try to create a quick summary of the passage in the box provided. Don't worry about writing in complete sentences, etc. Style is not important. Just try to identify the key points.

### *October 2002, Section 3, Passage 2*

Intellectual authority is defined as the authority of arguments that prevail by virtue of good reasoning and do not depend on coercion or convention. A contrasting notion, institutional authority, refers to the power of social institutions to enforce acceptance of arguments that may or may not possess intellectual authority. The authority wielded by legal systems is especially interesting because such systems are institutions that nonetheless aspire to a purely intellectual authority. One judge goes so far as to claim that courts are merely passive vehicles for applying intellectual authority of the law and possess no coercive powers of their own.

In contrast, some critics maintain that whatever authority judicial pronouncements have is exclusively institutional. Some of these critics go further, claiming that intellectual authority does not really exist—i.e., it reduces to institutional authority. But it can be countered that these claims break down when a sufficiently broad historical perspective is taken: Not all arguments accepted by institutions withstand the test of time, and some well-reasoned arguments never receive institutional imprimatur. The reasonable argument that goes unrecognized in its own time because it challenges institutional beliefs is common in intellectual history; intellectual authority and institutional consensus are not the same thing.

But, the critics might respond, intellectual authority is only recognized as such because of institutional consensus. For example, if a musicologist were to claim that an alleged musical genius who, after several decades, had not gained respect and recognition for his or her compositions is probably not a genius, the critics might say that basing a judgement on a unit of time—"several decades"—is an institutional rather than an intellectual construct. What, the critics might ask,

makes a particular number of decades reasonable evidence by which to judge genius? The answer, of course, is nothing, except for the fact that such institutional procedures have proved useful to musicologists in making such distinctions in the past.

The analogous legal concept is the doctrine of precedent, i.e., a judge's merely deciding a case a certain way becoming a basis for deciding later cases the same way—a pure example of institutional authority. But the critics miss the crucial distinction that when a judicial decision is badly reasoned, or simply no longer applies in the face of evolving social standards or practices, the notion of intellectual authority is introduced: judges reconsider, revise, or in some cases throw out the decision. The conflict between intellectual and institutional authority in legal systems is thus played out in the reconsideration of decisions, leading one to draw the conclusion that legal systems contain a significant degree of intellectual authority even if the thrust of their power is predominantly institutional.

SUMMARY

# Recognizing the Argument

## A Look into the Future...

We'll get back to the passage on the previous page momentarily, but first, let's fast-forward into the future. Imagine yourself as a law student, a legal scholar. There you sit, poring through legal cases, frantically scribbling notes, wondering if your name will be cold-called in tomorrow's lecture. You have so many cases to read, and so little time.

While the reading will be challenging, and you'll often wonder if you'll be able to get through it all, your fundamental task for each case that you read can be thought of in very simple terms: your job will be to (1) clearly define the two sides of a central argument, or case, (2) make note of the parties that fall on each side of the argument, and (3) consider any evidence that is presented in support of either side.

This all makes good sense. After all, law school is designed to prepare you for a career in law. In order for a lawyer or judge to successfully prepare for a case, she must understand the two sides of a central argument in a clear and specific manner. This understanding creates the framework from which she can evaluate and organize the evidence and opinions that are presented.

It is no wonder, then, that the LSAT would test your ability to deconstruct a reading passage in just this way.

## Defining Your Perspective: Read Like a Law Student

Though LSAT Reading Comprehension passages vary a good deal in terms of subject matter, they are remarkably consistent when it comes to structure. Most LSAT passages contain the features that you would find in a standard legal case (though, fortunately, without all the legal language). Most passages will:

1. Give background information necessary to understand an argument.
2. Present two sides of an argument.
3. Provide evidence or support for one side, or both.

Think of your approach to reading LSAT passages as similar to that which you would use to understand and analyze a legal case. In short, think of yourself as a law student as you read. It is from this perspective that you will most effectively organize and understand the information presented.

## Visualizing the Scale

As you read any given LSAT passage, your top priority should be to identify, in a clear and specific way, the two sides of the argument. In doing so, it is helpful to imagine the two sides of a balance scale as representing the competing sides of the argument.

For example:

**Some passages will give equal consideration to both sides of an argument.**

**2**

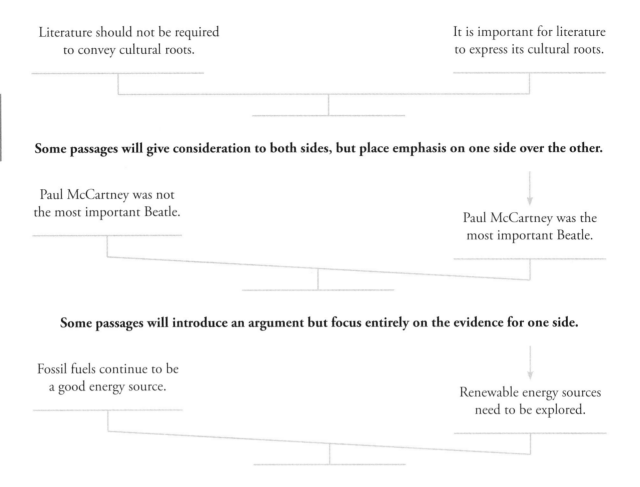

Literature should not be required
to convey cultural roots.

It is important for literature
to express its cultural roots.

**Some passages will give consideration to both sides, but place emphasis on one side over the other.**

Paul McCartney was not
the most important Beatle.

Paul McCartney was the
most important Beatle.

**Some passages will introduce an argument but focus entirely on the evidence for one side.**

Fossil fuels continue to be
a good energy source.

Renewable energy sources
need to be explored.

**Occasionally these passages will use the argument as a springboard to a related topic.** For example, a passage that starts out, "Renewable energy sources need to be explored," may go on to talk about one specific method of utilizing solar energy, and the positives and negatives of that particular method.

The two sides of the argument will provide you with a frame for "hanging" all of the other elements of the passage. *Everything* else in the passage exists in order to inform the sides of the argument in some way. In short, the scale image provides a simple approach for organizing the elements of the passage as you read.

In the next chapter, we'll look more closely at this concept of using the scale to organize your reading.

## The Curveballs

Every now and again you'll see a passage that deviates from the standard argument structure. Here are the most common curveball types:

**1. Strictly informative.** A few rare passages will not contain an argument at all. These passages are similar perhaps to what a law student might read for background information. These passages tend to be objective in nature, without opinion or emotion. Because of that, these passages will tend to

MANHATTAN
LSAT

be structured so as to give the reader information in an organized way, rather than in the conflicting manner of an argument. Often these passages are structured chronologically (perhaps the passage describes changes to the interpretation of a law at different periods in a country's history) or by logical necessity (perhaps it describes the workings of an artificial protein by discussing its individual parts).

**2. Two sides, but not opposing.** There have also been a couple of instances in the past few years where the two sides of an LSAT argument are somewhat conflicting but not opposites. For example, certain critics might say that a new law is flawed because it negatively impacts workers. Others say the law is flawed because it negatively impacts managers. In these instances, it is helpful to understand, going into the questions, that these are not opposing arguments, and that these opinions may play supporting roles in a bigger argument (that the new law is flawed).

Overall, however, the vast majority of passages that have appeared on the LSAT in the past 10 years have centered around a debatable argument. Finding the argument, and using it to mentally organize the passage, will make the reading process much easier. In the rare cases above, recognizing that an argument *isn't* present will generally give you an advantage when it comes to answering the questions.

# The Challenges of Recognizing the Argument

It can sometimes take lawyers and judges weeks or months to identify the crucial argument in a case. Fortunately for you, the LSAT isn't given over the course of weeks. Still, the test writers like to to challenge you by making the argument difficult to find. Here are two tips to help you overcome such obstacles:

**1. The central argument will not necessarily be revealed at the start of the passage.**

Remember that, in general terms, LSAT passages:

1. Give background information necessary to understand the argument.
2. Present the argument.
3. Provide evidence or support for one side, or both.

Unfortunately, the LSAT does not always give us passages written in this order. In fact, as the passages become more difficult, the three elements tend to get more and more mixed up. Do NOT use physical structure to anticipate where the meat of the argument is. Rather, maintain some flexibility as you search for the fundamental debate in the passage.

Here is a visual representation of three different ways in which a passage might be structured. These are representative of what you might see on the exam, but this is certainly not an exhaustive list of possibilities. The gray boxes represent paragraphs:

**EXAMPLE #1**

Background Information

_____

One side of argument (A)

Opposite side of
argument (B)

_____

Evidence for B

_____

Refutation/Evidence
for A

Evidence for A

**EXAMPLE #2**

One side of argument (A)

_____

Evidence for A

Background Information

Opposite side of
argument (B)

_____

Evidence for B

Evidence for B

**EXAMPLE #3**

Background Information

_____

Evidence for A

_____

Evidence for B

Background Information

_____

One side of argument (A)

Opposite side of
argument (B)

_____

Evidence for B

**2. The Argument is NOT to be confused with a comparison.** In a challenging passage, it is easy to confuse a comparison with an argument. What's the difference? Let's use an analogy you may have heard once or twice before in your life:

On one side you have apples and . . .          . . . on the other side oranges.

Is this an argument? Absolutely not. You can compare apples and oranges, but they are not two sides of an argument. If one person debates, "Apples!" and the other, "Oranges!" you would be listening to an illogical argument.

Now, let's think of some logical arguments we can make using apples and oranges:

*"Apples taste better than oranges."*
*"Oranges don't taste as sweet as apples."*
*"Apples are healthier for children than oranges are."*

Notice, all of these arguments are debatable, involve an opinion, and contain two sides. Furthermore, they all involve an action: "taste, don't taste, are." Let's revisit the beginning part of the passage that appeared at the start of the chapter:

**2**

**Passage:**

Intellectual authority is defined as the authority of arguments that prevail by virtue of good reasoning and do not depend on coercion or convention. A contrasting notion, institutional authority, refers to the power of social institutions to enforce acceptance of arguments that may or may not possess intellectual authority.

**Comment:**

*The passage begins by COMPARING intellectual authority and institutional authority, but it would be a mistake to assign those ideas, in and of themselves, to opposite sides of an argument. They are contrasting ideas, but we have yet to be introduced to a debate. We can consider this background information.*

*Rushing to judgment at this point leads to the following INCORRECT scale analysis:*

Intellectual authority                                    Institutional authority

The authority wielded by legal systems is especially interesting because such systems are institutions that nonetheless aspire to a purely intellectual authority.

*This is more background information that narrows down the scope of the argument. Now we have an arena, "legal systems," for these contrasting ideas to square off in.*

One judge goes so far as to claim that courts are merely passive vehicles for applying intellectual authority of the
law and possess no coercive powers of their own.

*This is the first concrete opinion that has been presented: one judge claims that courts are vehicles for intellectual authority, and have no institutional authority.*

Courts apply intellectual
authority only.

In contrast, some critics maintain that whatever authority judicial pronouncements have is exclusively institutional . . .

*We could probably anticipate this before we get to this point. An opposing opinion is presented: some critics say that the power of legal systems is purely institutional. Now we have the two sides of our central argument.*

Courts apply intellectual
authority only.

The power of courts is
purely institutional.

At this point, take a look back at the passage summary you wrote on the first page of the chapter and compare it with this scale. The central argument is the most important information in a passage, and your notes should reflect that.

When you read a real LSAT argument, you should not try to draw this scale. However, it is a useful mental structure to train yourself to use.

Let's get some practice looking for the central argument and the two sides of the scale.

# DRILL IT: Recognizing the Argument

Each of the following is a truncated version of a real reading passage that has appeared on a past LSAT. Give yourself one minute per passage. Your goal is to correctly identify the two sides of the argument.

### October 2002, Section 3, Passage 1

The myth persists that in 1492 the Western Hemisphere was an untamed wilderness and that it was European settlers who harnessed and transformed its ecosystems. But scholarship shows that forests, in particular, had been altered to varying degrees well before the arrival of Europeans. Native populations had converted much of the forests to successfully cultivated stands, especially by means of burning. Nevertheless, some researchers have maintained that the extent, frequency, and impact of such burning was minimal. However, a large body of evidence for the routine practice of burning exists in the geographical record. One group of researchers found, for example, that sedimentary charcoal accumulations in what is now the northeastern United States are greatest where known native American settlements were greatest.

### December 2002, Section 3, Passage 3

With the approach of the twentieth century, the classical wave theory of radiation—a widely accepted theory in physics—began to encounter obstacles. One fundamental assumption of wave theory was that as the length of a wave of radiation shortens, its energy increases smoothly—like a volume dial on a radio that adjusts smoothly to any setting—and that any conceivable energy value could thus occur in nature. Max Planck, a classical physicist who made important contributions to wave theory, discarded the assumption of radiation's smooth energy continuum and took the then bizarre position that these atomic processes could only involve discrete energies that jump between certain units of value—like a volume dial that "clicks" between incremental settings. The physics community was at first quite critical of Planck's hypothesis, in part because he presented it without physical explanation. Soon thereafter, however, Albert Einstein and other physicists provided theoretical justification for Planck's hypothesis.

### June 2002, Section 1, Passage 1

A crucial component of the jury trial, at least in serious criminal cases, is the rule that verdicts be unanimous among the jurors. Under this requirement, dissenting jurors must either be convinced of the rightness of the prevailing opinion, or, conversely, persuade the other jurors to change their minds. In either instance, the unanimity requirement compels the jury to deliberate fully and truly before reaching its verdict. Critics of the unanimity requirement, however, see it as a costly relic that extends the deliberation process and sometimes, in a hung jury, brings it to a halt. But the material costs of hung juries do not warrant losing the benefit to society of the unanimous verdict. Requiring unanimity provides a better chance that a trial, and thus a verdict, will be fair.

### December 2002, Section 3, Passage 1

The contemporary Mexican artistic movement known as muralism, a movement of public art that began with images painted on walls in an effort to represent Mexican national culture, is closely linked ideologically with its main sponsor, the new Mexican government elected in 1920 following the Mexican Revolution. This government promoted an ambitious cultural program, and the young revolutionary state called on artists to display Mexico's richness and possibility. But the theoretical foundation of the movement was formulated by the artists themselves. While many muralist works express populist or nationalist ideas, it is a mistake to attempt to reduce Mexican mural painting to formulaic, official government art. It is more than merely the result of the changes in political and social awareness that the Mexican Revolution represented; it also reflected important innovations in the art world. Awareness of these innovations enabled these artists to be freer in expression than were more traditional practitioners of this style.

**2**

How does the brain know when carbohydrates have been or should be consumed? The answer to this question is not known, but one element in the explanation seems to be the neurotransmitter serotonin, one of a class of chemical mediators that may be released from a presynaptic neuron and that cause the transmission of nerve impulse across a synapse to an adjacent postsynaptic neuron. In general, it has been found that drugs that selectively facilitate serotonin-mediated neurotransmission tend to cause weight loss, whereas drugs that block serotonin-mediated transmission often have the opposite effect: they often induce carbohydrate craving and consequent weight gain.

Serotonin is a derivative of tryptophan, an amino acid that is normally present at low levels in the bloodstream. The rate of conversion is affected by the proportion of carbohydrates in an individual's diet: carbohydrates stimulate the secretion of insulin, which facilitates the uptake of most amino acids into peripheral tissues, such as muscles. Blood tryptophan levels, however, are unaffected by insulin, so the proportion of tryptophan in the blood relative to the other amino acids increases when carbohydrates are consumed. Since tryptophan competes with other amino acids for the transport across the blood-brain barrier into the brain, insulin secretion indirectly speeds tryptophan's entry into the central nervous system, where, in a special cluster of neurons, it is converted into serotonin.

# SOLUTIONS: Recognizing the Argument

The parts of the passage that inform us of the central argument have been underlined.

**2**

### *October 2002, Section 3, Passage 1*

The myth persists that in 1492 the Western Hemisphere was an untamed wilderness and that it was European settlers who harnessed and transformed its ecosystems. But scholarship shows that forests, in particular, had been altered to varying degrees well before the arrival of Europeans. Native populations had converted much of the forests to successfully cultivated stands, especially by means of burning. Nevertheless, some researchers have maintained that the extent, frequency, and impact of such burning was minimal. However, a large body of evidence for the routine practice of burning exists in the geographical record. One group of researchers found, for example, that sedimentary charcoal accumulations in what is now the northeastern United States are greatest where known native American settlements were greatest.

**Side A:**
Western Hemisphere was untamed wilderness before European settlers, and they were first to harness and transform ecosystems. (Note: Later, this opinion gets softened a bit, with researchers acknowledging that Native Americans might have altered the land slightly, but that the overall effect was minimal.)

**Side B:**
Western Hemisphere ecosystems, particularly forests, were altered by humans well before arrival of Europeans. (Note: The author's opinion is made clear through a shift in wording. The first opinion is characterized as a "myth," while the second is written with authority, "scholarship shows . . ." )

### *December 2002, Section 3, Passage 3*

With the approach of the twentieth century, the classical wave theory of radiation—a widely accepted theory in physics—began to encounter obstacles. One fundamental assumption of wave theory was that as the length of a wave of radiation shortens, its energy increases smoothly—like a volume dial on a radio that adjusts smoothly to any setting—and that any conceivable energy value could thus occur in nature. Max Planck, a classical physicist who made important contributions to wave theory, discarded the assumption of radiation's smooth energy continuum and took the then bizarre position that these atomic processes could only involve discrete energies that jump between certain units of value—like a volume dial that "clicks" between incremental settings. The physics community was at first quite critical of Planck's hypothesis, in part because he presented it without physical explanation. Soon thereafter, however, Albert Einstein and other physicists provided theoretical justification for Planck's hypothesis.

**Side A:**
Classical Wave theory is correct.

**Side B:**
Classical Wave theory is incorrect.

Here the argument is not clearly spelled out. In the first sentence, a theory on how radiation waves function is introduced and immediately put into doubt. The rest of the passage supports the second opinion, and is presented with an objective tone that tells us that his opinion can be considered fact.

**2**

### June 2002, Section 1, Passage 1

A crucial component of the jury trial, at least in serious criminal cases, is the rule that verdicts be unanimous among the jurors. Under this requirement, dissenting jurors must either be convinced of the rightness of the prevailing opinion, or, conversely, persuade the other jurors to change their minds. In either instance, the unanimity requirement compels the jury to deliberate fully and truly before reaching its verdict. Critics of the unanimity requirement, however, see it as a costly relic that extends the deliberation process and sometimes, in a hung jury, brings it to a halt. But the material costs of hung juries do not warrant losing the benefit to society of the unanimous verdict. Requiring unanimity provides a better chance that a trial, and thus a verdict, will be fair.

**Side A:**
The jury trial is a costly relic that slows down the trial process.

**Side B:**
The benefits of jury trials outweigh the costs.

### December 2002, Section 3, Passage 1

The contemporary Mexican artistic movement known as muralism, a movement of public art that began with images painted on walls in an effort to represent Mexican national culture, is closely linked ideologically with its main sponsor, the new Mexican government elected in 1920 following the Mexican Revolution. This government promoted an ambitious cultural program, and the young revolutionary state called on artists to display Mexico's richness and possibility. But the theoretical foundation of the movement was formulated by the artists themselves. While many muralist works express populist or nationalist ideas, it is a mistake to attempt to reduce Mexican mural painting to formulaic, official government art. It is more than merely the result of the changes in political and social awareness that the Mexican Revolution represented; it also reflected important innovations in the art world. Awareness of these innovations enabled these artists to be freer in expression than were more traditional practitioners of this style.

**Side A:**
Mexican mural painting is formulaic, official government art.

**Side B:**
Mexican mural painting is more than that; it also reflected important innovations in the art world.

*Note: The first sentence of the passage sounds like it could be the introduction of an argument (perhaps some others don't think that the mural movement is closely linked to government ideology), but it turns out otherwise because the other side of that potential argument is never presented. Rather, the argument turns out to be about something more specific and subtle—the author acknowledges the connection between the two, but makes a claim that political ideology isn't the only influence.*

## October 1994, Section 3, Passage 4

How does the brain know when carbohydrates have been or should be consumed? The answer to this question is not known, but one element in the explanation seems to be the neurotransmitter serotonin, one of a class of chemical mediators that may be released from a presynaptic neuron and that cause the transmission of nerve impulse across a synapse to an adjacent postsynaptic neuron. In general, it has been found that drugs that selectively facilitate serotonin-mediated neurotransmission tend to cause weight loss, whereas drugs that block serotonin-mediated transmission often have the opposite effect: they often induce carbohydrate craving and consequent weight gain.

Serotonin is a derivative of tryptophan, an amino acid that is normally present at low levels in the bloodstream. The rate of conversion is affected by the proportion of carbohydrates in an individual's diet: carbohydrates stimulate the secretion of insulin, which facilitates the uptake of most amino acids into peripheral tissues, such as muscles. Blood tryptophan levels, however, are unaffected by insulin, so the proportion of tryptophan in the blood relative to the other amino acids increases when carbohydrates are consumed. Since tryptophan competes with other amino acids for the transport across the blood-brain barrier into the brain, insulin secretion indirectly speeds tryptophan's entry into the central nervous system, where, in a special cluster of neurons, it is converted into serotonin.

**CURVEBALL: Strictly Informative**

There is no argument here at all! Notice that all the information is presented in an objective, unemotional manner. Not even the author expresses an opinion.

*Note: Even when a passage lacks a clear argument, reading like a law student is useful. By actively seeking the argument, and by attempting to anticipate what the argument might turn out to be at different points in the passage, you are keeping yourself actively engaged in the reading process. This in and of itself will lead to higher levels of comprehension.*

2

# Chapter 3

## of

## Reading Comprehension

# Using the Argument as a Framework

# Reading Like a Law Student

Is it enough to come away from your first read of an LSAT passage with just an understanding of the central argument? Can you ignore the rest of the passage? Unfortunately, no.

Use the argument as a framework that allows you to correctly interpret and organize the entire passage. **That is, consider every piece of the passage carefully in terms of the role it could play relative to the central argument.**

Let's define all of the roles that different parts of the passage can play:

**1. Background information.** In general, LSAT passages will involve topics that the typical reader will know little or nothing about. Think of the background information as a platform or playing field for the argument. Background information is generally given at the beginning of a passage, but it is not limited to the beginning of the passage.

**2. The argument itself.** Beware of the difference between two comparable elements and two sides of a debate or argument. Sometimes the argument is clear; other times it is subtle and well hidden within the text, and sometimes it unravels itself within a few different parts. Don't rush to judgment. The *process* of peeling away the layers, and searching for the exact issue at hand, should make you a stronger reader.

**3. Opinions.** The opinions presented in a text will support one side of the argument or the other. Some opinions will be assigned to vague, general groups, such as "critics" and "lawyers," while others will be accredited to specific individuals. Questions are often built around opinions presented in the text, and in these cases it is imperative to have a clear understanding of which side of the argument an opinion falls on. Of course, the most important opinion is . . .

**The author's opinion,** which may be clearly given, or stated subtly, perhaps implicitly. LSAT passages are never written in the first person; often, the author's opinion is made clear because it is implicitly the opinion of the passage itself. For example, consider the statement, "Critics find Carver's work derivative and simplistic, but they are clearly wrong." In this case, it is clear that the author's opinion is the opposite of that of the critics. Almost all passages contain an author's opinion, and it is a top priority for you to identify it and assign it to the correct side of the argument.

**4. Evidence that supports one side of the argument.** This evidence can be theoretical, such as the idea that great literature should be emotionally moving, or it can be factual, such as the existence of genetic proof of mutations. Evidence that goes against an opinion can be considered evidence for the other side of the argument.

**5. The curved tail.** Once in a while, there will be a section that plays none of these roles. Often, these "curveball" elements come at the end of a passage, and take us into some tangential discussion, outside the immediate scope of the central argument.

# DRILL IT: Using the Argument as a Framework

Following are some of the same truncated LSAT texts from the drill in the previous chapter. This time, they have been separated into individual sentences. Your task is to correctly recognize the role each sentence plays in the overall argument. Note that it may be difficult to categorize a particular sentence until you've read more of the passage.

**The possible roles are: Background information, Both sides of the argument, One side of the argument (A), The other side of the argument (B), Support for A, Support for B. Sometimes a sentence will play multiple roles. Feel free to use your own shorthand if you'd like.**

3

*October 2002, Section 3, Passage 1*

(1) The myth persists that in 1492 the Western Hemisphere was an untamed wilderness and that it was European settlers who harnessed and transformed its ecosystems.        _____

(2) But scholarship shows that forests, in particular, had been altered to varying degrees well before the arrival of Europeans.        _____

(3) Native populations had converted much of the forests to successfully cultivated stands, especially by means of burning.        _____

(4) Nevertheless, some researchers have maintained that the extent, frequency, and impact of such burning was minimal.        _____

(5) However, a large body of evidence for the routine practice of burning exists in the geographical record.        _____

(6) One group of researchers found, for example, that sedimentary charcoal accumulations in what is now the northeastern United States are greatest where known native American settlements were greatest.        _____

*December 2002, Section 3, Passage 3*

(1) With the approach of the twentieth century, the classical wave theory of radiation—a widely accepted theory in physics—began to encounter obstacles.        _____

(2) One fundamental assumption of wave theory was that as the length of a wave of radiation shortens, its energy increases smoothly—like a volume dial on a radio that adjusts smoothly to any setting—and that any conceivable energy value could thus occur in nature.        _____

(3) Max Planck, a classical physicist who made important contributions to wave theory, discarded the assumption of radiation's smooth energy continuum and took the then bizarre position that these atomic processes could only involve discrete energies that jump between certain unites of value— like a volume dial that "clicks" between incremental settings.        _____

(4) The physics community was at first quite critical of Planck's hypothesis, in part because he presented it without physical explanation.        _____

(5) Soon thereafter, however, Albert Einstein and other physicists provided theoretical justification for Planck's hypothesis.        _____

**The possible roles are: Background information, Both sides of the argument, One side of the argument (A), The other side of the argument (B), Support for A, Support for B. Sometimes a sentence will play multiple roles. Feel free to use your own shorthand if you'd like.**

### *June 2002, Section 1, Passage 1*

(1) A crucial component of the jury trial, at least in serious criminal cases, is the rule that verdicts be unanimous among the jurors.

_____

(2) Under this requirement, dissenting jurors must either be convinced of the rightness of the prevailing opinion, or, conversely, persuade the other jurors to change their minds.

_____

(3) In either instance, the unanimity requirement compels the jury to deliberate fully and truly before reaching its verdict.

_____

(4) Critics of the unanimity requirement, however, see it as a costly relic that extends the deliberation process and sometimes, in a hung jury, brings it to a halt.

_____

(5) But the material costs of hung juries do not warrant losing the benefit to society of the unanimous verdict.

_____

(6) Requiring unanimity provides a better chance that a trial, and thus a verdict, will be fair.

_____

### *December 2002, Section 3, Passage 1*

(1) The contemporary Mexican artistic movement known as muralism, a movement of public art that began with images painted on walls in an effort to represent Mexican national culture, is closely linked ideologically with its main sponsor, the new Mexican government elected in 1920 following the Mexican Revolution.

_____

(2) This government promoted an ambitious cultural program, and the young revolutionary state called on artists to display Mexico's richness and possibility.

_____

(3) But the theoretical foundation of the movement was formulated by the artists themselves. While many muralist works express populist or nationalist ideas, it is a mistake to attempt to reduce Mexican mural painting to formulaic, official government art.

_____

(4) It is more than merely the result of the changes in political and social awareness that the Mexican Revolution represented; it also reflected important innovations in the art world.

_____

(5) Awareness of these innovations enabled these artists to be freer in expression than were more traditional practitioners of this style.

_____

# SOLUTIONS: Using the Argument as a Framework

As we mentioned, it may be difficult to categorize a particular sentence until you've read more of the passage. The first passage is a good example. We can't really determine that Sentence (1) is one side of the argument until we've read Sentence (2).

Also, it's less important that you've categorized each sentence in exactly the same way that we have; what's more important is that you've identified the two sides of the argument, and that you've assigned the opinions (especially that of the author) and evidence to the correct sides.

Finally, keep in mind that the scale image is meant to be a way for you to mentally organize the material, and not necessarily a physical note-taking method. While writing out the scale for practice is a good way to get accustomed to thinking in this manner, physically doing so during the exam would be impractical. Later, we'll discuss annotation techniques that you can use during the exam to help you think through the scale image in real time.

### *October 2002, Section 3, Passage 1*

(1) The myth persists that in 1492 the Western Hemisphere was an untamed wilderness and that it was European settlers who harnessed and transformed its ecosystems.

**One side of the argument (A)**

(2) But scholarship shows that forests, in particular, had been altered to varying degrees well before the arrival of Europeans.

**Other side of the argument (B)**

(3) Native populations had converted much of the forests to successfully cultivated stands, especially by means of burning.

**Support for B**

(4) Nevertheless, some researchers have maintained that the extent, frequency, and impact of such burning was minimal.

**Support for A**

(5) However, a large body of evidence for the routine practice of burning exists in the geographical record.

**Support for B**

(6) One group of researchers found, for example, that sedimentary charcoal accumulations in what is now the northeastern United States are greatest where known native American settlements were greatest.

**Support for B**

**Western Hemisphere was untamed wilderness before European settlers, and they were first to harness and transform ecosystems.**

**Western Hemisphere ecosystems, particularly forests, altered by humans well before arrival of Europeans.**

Opinions for:
Prevailing myth, some researchers

Support for:
-Burning minimal

Opinions for:
Scholarship, **AUTHOR**, one group of researchers

Support for:
-Native populations converted forests to cultivated lands through burning
-Large body of evidence for routine burning in geographical record
-Charcoal accumulation greatest where there were most settlements

### December 2002, Section 3, Passage 3

(1) With the approach of the twentieth century, the classical wave theory of radiation—a widely accepted theory in physics—began to encounter obstacles.

**Background information, Both sides of the argument**
_____

(2) One fundamental assumption of wave theory was that as the length of a wave of radiation shortens, its energy increases smoothly—like a volume dial on a radio that adjusts smoothly to any setting—and that any conceivable energy value could thus occur in nature.

**One side of the argument (A)**
_____

(3) Max Planck, a classical physicist who made important contributions to wave theory, discarded the assumption of radiation's smooth energy continuum and took the then bizarre position that these atomic processes could only involve discrete energies that jump between certain unites of value—like a volume dial that "clicks" between incremental settings.

**Other side of the argument (B)**
_____

(4) The physics community was at first quite critical of Planck's hypothesis, in part because he presented it without physical explanation.

**Support for A**
_____

(5) Soon thereafter, however, Albert Einstein and other physicists provided theoretical justification for Planck's hypothesis.

**Support for B**
_____

**Classical wave theory is correct.**

**Classical wave theory is incorrect.**

Opinions for:

Max Planck, **AUTHOR**, Albert Einstein, other physicists

Opinions for:
Physics community at first

Support for:

-MP disproves foundation of classical wave theory
-AE provides justification for MP proof

**\* Note here that the scale is weighted more on one side, because most of the passage is about why classical wave theory is incorrect.**

3

**_June 2002, Section 1, Passage 1_**

| | |
|---|---|
| (1) A crucial component of the jury trial, at least in serious criminal cases, is the rule that verdicts be unanimous among the jurors. | **Background information** |
| (2) Under this requirement, dissenting jurors must either be convinced of the rightness of the prevailing opinion, or, conversely, persuade the other jurors to change their minds. | **Background information** |
| (3) In either instance, the unanimity requirement compels the jury to deliberate fully and truly before reaching its verdict. | **Background information, Support for B** |
| (4) Critics of the unanimity requirement, however, see it as a costly relic that extends the deliberation process and sometimes, in a hung jury, brings it to a halt. | **One side of the argument (A)** |
| (5) But the material costs of hung juries do not warrant losing the benefit to society of the unanimous verdict. | **Other side of the argument (B)** |
| (6) Requiring unanimity provides a better chance that a trial, and thus a verdict, will be fair. | **Support for B** |

**Jury trial is a costly relic that slows down the trial process.**

**The benefits of jury trials outweigh the costs.**

Opinions for:
Critics

Support for:
-Delays process

Opinions for:
**AUTHOR**

Support for:
-Forces jury to deliberate fully
-Provides better chance that the trial is fair

***December 2002, Section 3, Passage 1***

(1) The contemporary Mexican artistic movement known as muralism, a movement of public art that began with images painted on walls in an effort to represent Mexican national culture, is closely linked ideologically with its main sponsor, the new Mexican government elected in 1920 following the Mexican Revolution.

**Background information**

(2) This government promoted an ambitious cultural program, and the young revolutionary state called on artists to display Mexico's richness and possibility.

**Background information**

(3) But the theoretical foundation of the movement was formulated by the artists themselves. While many muralist works express populist or nationalist ideas, it is a mistake to attempt to reduce Mexican mural painting to formulaic, official government art.

**Background information, Both sides of the argument**

(4) It is more than merely the result of the changes in political and social awareness that the Mexican Revolution represented; it also reflected important innovations in the art world.

**One side of the argument (A)**

(5) Awareness of these innovations enabled these artists to be freer in expression than were more traditional practitioners of this style.

**Support for A**

**Mexican mural painting is more than that; it also reflected important innovations in the art world.**

**Mexican mural painting is formulaic official government art.**

Opinions for:
**AUTHOR**

Support for:
-Innovations enable artists to be freer in expression

# Putting It All Together

In the last chapter, we looked at a complete LSAT passage and began to define the argument contained within it. Now, let's reread the passage, this time using the argument as a framework for understanding the passage as a whole.

### October 2002, Section 3, Passage 2

**Comment:**

Intellectual authority is defined as the authority of arguments that prevail by virtue of good reasoning and do not depend on coercion or convention. A contrasting notion, institutional authority, refers to the power of social institutions to enforce acceptance of arguments that may or may not possess intellectual authority.

*This is background information. Institutional and intellectual authority are introduced as contrasting elements (like apples and oranges) but they are not two different sides of a debate.*

The authority wielded by legal systems is especially interesting because such systems are institutions that nonetheless aspire to a purely intellectual authority.

*Still background information. Now we are narrowing in on a specific subject area where these contrasting notions come into conflict: legal systems.*

*One side of the argument is presented (A): legal systems apply pure intellectual authority.*

One judge goes so far as to claim that courts are merely passive vehicles for applying intellectual authority of the law and possess no coercive powers of their own.

In contrast, some critics maintain that whatever authority judicial pronouncements have is exclusively institutional.

*The opposing side is presented (B): power of legal systems is exclusively institutional. Now we know the two sides of the argument.*

Some of these critics go further, claiming that intellectual authority does not really exist—i.e., it reduces to institutional authority.

*Support for, and expansion of (B)*

*Counterargument that supports (A).*

But it can be countered that these claims break down when a sufficiently broad historical perspective is taken: Not all arguments accepted by institutions withstand the test of time, and some well-reasoned arguments never receive institutional imprimatur. The reasonable argument that goes unrecognized in its own time because it challenges institutional beliefs is common in intellectual history;

*Notice the structure and tone. **This is the author's opinion**. The author sides with intellectual authority (A).*

intellectual authority and institutional consensus are not the same thing.

**Passage**

**Comment:**

But, the critics might respond, intellectual authority is only recognized as such because of institutional consensus. For example, if a musicologist were to claim that an alleged musical genius who, after several decades, had not gained respect and recognition for his or her compositions is probably not a genius, the critics might say that basing a judgement on a unit of time—"several decades"—is an institutional rather than an intellectual construct. What, the critics might ask, makes a particular number of decades reasonable evidence by which to judge genius? The answer, of course, is nothing, except for the fact that such institutional procedures have proved useful to musicologists in making such distinctions in the past.

*Support for opinion B, institutional authority.*

The analogous legal concept is the doctrine of precedent, i.e., a judge's merely deciding a case a certain way becoming a basis for deciding later cases the same way—a pure example of institutional authority.

*Support for opinion B.*

But the critics miss the crucial distinction that when a judicial decision is badly reasoned, or simply no longer applies in the face of evolving social standards or practices, the notion of intellectual authority is introduced: judges reconsider, revise, or in some cases throw out the decision. The conflict between intellectual and institutional authority in legal systems is thus played out in the reconsideration of decisions, leading one to draw the conclusion that legal systems contain a significant degree of intellectual authority even if the thrust of their power is predominantly institutional.

*Counterargument that supports opinion A. Notice a slight softening of the stance—though the author believes in the impact of intellectual authority and is clearly on one side of this debate, his or her opinion is not as absolute as the one given by the judge at the end of paragraph one.*

This is an extremely difficult passage. The subject matter is most likely unfamiliar, the language is challenging, and the flow of the passage seems to change directions often. The best way to make sense of this passage is to organize the information according to the central argument. Mentally "hang" each passage component on your scale image as you read.

### A Visual Representation

If we put the argument and the related pieces on a scale, it might look like this:

Background:
Intellectual Authority: authority because of reason
Institutional Authority: authority because of authority (i.e., without reason)

**The power of legal
systems is institutional.**

**3**

**The power of legal
systems is intellectual.**

Opinions:
-Critics

Support:
-Critics: purely institutional
-Institutional/Intellectual authority is same
-Basing judgment on unit of time (in musicology) makes it institutional
-Precedent is example of institutional authority

Opinions:
-Judge
-**AUTHOR**

Support:
-Judge: purely intellectual
-Institutional/Intellectual authority is not same
-The way judges can go against precedent shows power of intellectual authority

Again, it is unnecessary (and too time consuming) to write out this scale on the actual exam, but you want to understand the passage well enough so that, if asked to, you *could* create this scale. If you can come away from every passage on the LSAT with this type of understanding, you will be in terrific position for answering the types of questions that appear on the exam.

# The Benefits of Reading Like a Law Student

In the second half of the book, we will specifically discuss how reading like a law student gives you an advantage when it comes to answering particular types of questions, but let's pause for a moment and quickly highlight some of the benefits of this type of reading stance.

**1. The method is a natural fit for the structure of the passages.** As mentioned earlier, these passages are designed to test the very same reading and recognition skills that will be required in law school, which in turn attempt to mimic the skills that will be required of you as a lawyer, or as a judge. **These passages are meant to be read this way.** Furthermore, remember that the constant in all the exam passages is not the *subject matter* but rather the *structure*; if you are prepared for what you are going to read, and understand each element of a passage in terms of the passage's overall structure, you will read faster and retain more than you would going into this exam with a blank slate.

**2. Most general questions depend on a clear understanding of the central argument in the passage.** If you can divide the passage into the two sides of the scale, you will be ready to answer most questions that pertain to the passage as a whole. Also, general questions will often require you to correctly incorporate and assign the various opinions, especially those of the author.

Let's look at a question that pertains to the passage we've been discussing:

*October 2002, Section 3, Passage 2, #9*

9. Which one of the following most accurately states the main idea of the passage?

(A) Although some argue that the authority of legal systems is purely intellectual, these systems possess a degree of institutional authority due to their ability to enforce acceptance of badly reasoned or socially inappropriate judicial decisions.

(B) Although some argue that the authority of legal systems is purely institutional, these systems are more correctly seen as vehicles for applying the intellectual authority of the law while possessing no coercive power of their own.

(C) Although some argue that the authority of legal systems is purely intellectual, these systems in fact wield institutional authority by virtue of the fact that intellectual authority reduces to institutional authority.

(D) Although some argue that the authority of legal systems is purely institutional, these systems possess a degree of intellectual authority due to their ability to reconsider badly reasoned or socially inappropriate judicial decisions.

(E) Although some argue that the authority of legal systems is purely intellectual, these systems in fact wield exclusively institutional authority in that they possess the power to enforce acceptance of badly reasoned or socially inappropriate judicial decisions.

Notice the structure of the answer choices: each answer starts with an "although," and then gives us an opinion that is attributed to a vague group, "some"; next, an alternate opinion is given that clearly represents the author's opinion. When we think about our scale in these terms, the answer should read (in a general sense):

> "Although some think the power of legal systems is institutional, it is intellectual."

Based on this general understanding, we can quickly eliminate answer choices (A), (C), and (E), which incorrectly represent the argument in reverse.

Left with (B) and (D), let's examine the remaining choices in more depth. (B) may initially sound correct, but it is too extreme when it asserts that it has "no coercive power." Though the author is on the side of intellectual power, her feelings are not that absolute. She ends the passage noting that "legal systems contain a significant degree of intellectual authority even if the thrust of their power is predominantly institutional."

Answer choice (D) is correct. The ability of courts to reconsider bad judgments was a significant piece of evidence that fell on the same side as the author's opinion.

Is answer choice (D) a perfect summary of the passage? No. It doesn't accurately represent the priorities of the author. However, it is clearly the best of the available answer choices.

**3. Specific questions often depend on an understanding of the *role* played by a piece of information in the passage.** Let's look at a specific question:

**3**

> *October 2002, Section 3, Passage 2, #13*
>
> 13.  The author discusses the example from musicology primarily
>      in order to
>
> (A)  distinguish the notion of institutional authority from that of
>      intellectual authority.
> (B)  give an example of an argument possessing intellectual authority
>      that did not prevail in its own time.
> (C)  identify an example in which the ascription of musical genius
>      did not withstand the test of time.
> (D)  illustrate the claim that assessing intellectual authority requires
>      an appeal to institutional authority.
> (E)  demonstrate that the authority wielded by the arbiters of musical
>      genius is entirely institutional.

In order to answer a specific question successfully, you need to interpret a piece of text and understand its role in the argument. Look back at the scale. In this case, musicology is mentioned as an example that supports the claim made in the first sentence of the third paragraph: "But, the critics might respond, intellectual authority is only recognized as such because of institutional consensus."

The correct answer is (D).

# Chapter 4

## Reading Comprehension

# Passage Annotation and the Reading Process

# Passage Annotation

## The Purpose of Annotation

Ideally, you want to walk into the exam with an annotation system that you've practiced and feel very comfortable with. The process of annotating, or marking the passage with notes, will help you in several ways. For one, most of us read much more actively, and carefully, when we take notes. The very act of marking the passage forces us to make decisions about what information is important, and how parts of the passage relate to one another. As you are answering the questions, your notes should help reinforce the central concepts in the passage, and, more importantly, your notes should help you recall the thought processes you went through on your initial read.

All that said, passage annotation can quickly become counterproductive if you're not careful. We'll present our recommended annotation approaches in a minute, but first a few words of warning. As you work on your own annotation process, keep the following in mind:

**1. Annotation is a means to an end.** Never let the *process* of annotation become more important than actually *understanding* the passage. You must remember that the process is meant to serve your understanding of the central argument and its associated parts. The end goal is always comprehension. If your annotation process isn't helping you understand the central argument, then you need to change your process.

**2. There is no such thing as correct or incorrect annotation.** Each of us will annotate differently, meaning that each of us will end up with a unique set of notes. Again, the annotation in and of itself is not what's important. Rather, you should evaluate your notating system in terms of how much it helps you read more carefully, and how much it helps you retain information more easily.

**3. Your annotation will be a record of your *evolving* understanding of the passage.** You may mark up the beginning of the passage based on some premature understanding of the central argument only to discover later that you need to revise that understanding. Does this mean that your initial markings are wrong or need to be erased? No! Leave them as is. Remember, you *should* be guessing and reassessing your understanding of the passage. That's part of the process. Let your notes be a record of your evolving understanding.

## The Process of Annotation

As we mentioned, there are many different ways to annotate, and everyone will have a different method that is most effective for them. Remember, whatever process you do decide to use, make sure you are practiced at it by test day.

Here are three suggestions for the annotation process:

**1. Underline and mark up as you read.** This is probably the most obvious method, but be careful: very few of us can underline effectively *as we read*. The reason is that it's very difficult to understand the meaning and purpose of a sentence without the context of knowing both what's come before it and what's coming after it.

MANHATTAN
LSAT

If you underline as you read, and you are not careful, it's easy to end up passively underlining too much, or getting into a rhythm and thinking you have to underline once every few sentences. It's easy to get distracted by the underlining, so that you lose focus of what you are reading.

Therefore, this method is effective only for a small percentage of test-takers. *Use this method only if it's clearly the one that feels most natural to you.* Generally, that's going to be if you are a very strong reader to begin with, and very selective when it comes to what items you are going to underline or notate (you tend to underline too little, rather than too much).

Here are some symbols you might want to use as part of your notation process:

(1) = one side of the argument          (2) = other side of the argument

(O₁) = opinion for one side          (O₂) = opinion for the other

(A) = author's opinion

Again, if other symbols make more sense to you, please feel free to use them. In any case, any notation system you use should be automatic for you by test day.

**2. Underline and mark up at the end of each paragraph.** This is the method we recommend for most test-takers. Once you are done with a paragraph, skim it quickly and decide on what is most important, and what is worthy of taking note of. Then use the same underlining and symbol process we just discussed. This method naturally builds in a review process we'll discuss shortly.

**3. Take notes on the side.** Writing notes in your own words will take a little more time than underlining will. However, for some people, it's a much more natural process. In addition, putting ideas into your own words forces you to figure out what is most important, and what the text truly means. Furthermore, writing notes allows you to be more specific about the purpose of each part of the passage.

It might seem helpful to take notes in the form of a scale image. We've found that this is very difficult to do, and we don't generally recommend it. Remember, if you do decide to take notes, make sure the process doesn't slow you down too much.

## What to Notate

With any annotation process, the goal is to help you focus in on, and remember, the most important information. What is the most important information? It's the stuff we've been focused on in the past few chapters. At the end of the day, your annotation process should help you:

1. Figure out the central argument.
2. Assign opinions to different sides.
3. Recognize the purpose of all supporting information.

If you are underlining, you want to focus on sentences that inform you about numbers 1 and 2. These are the most important issues to understand completely. Essentially, this means that everything you don't underline is supporting evidence or background information. Though these parts will go unnotated, you should be able to see how these relate to the opinions and central argument that you do notate.

If you are taking notes on the side, you can note the central argument, opinions, *and* purpose of supporting information. It is unnecessary, and a waste of time, to summarize the *meaning* of the supporting evidence—you just want to notate its *purpose* relative to the argument.

# Project PEAR

Thus far in this chapter, we've discussed the physical processes you should go through while reading an LSAT passage. Now let's discuss some important mental processes.

You can use the acronym **PEAR** to remember these key steps necessary for being an effective reader:

### Pause

When people are asked to rush through the reading of a passage, to read faster than they would otherwise, they tend to cut out the time they spend pausing and reflecting on the material. This is a crucial mistake. We need these pauses to think about what we've read; without them, there's simply too much information for us to absorb. What often results is that we'll be able to understand the meaning of sentences only in relation to those immediately preceding or following, but not in relation to the passage as a whole.

The breaks between paragraphs are natural places to pause and reflect on the significance of what you've read. (It's also helpful to pause when you first encounter a sentence that hints at the central argument.)

Specifically, you want to pause at the end of each paragraph and…

### Evaluate

Evaluate what you've just read. Did anything clue you in on the central argument? Were there any opinions presented? Did the author tip his hand in terms of his own opinion? If so, review these ideas again, and try your best to connect them to one another. If you are not underlining as you read, this is a natural moment to underline and mark up, or to take notes.

And…

### Anticipate

Next, try to predict the various roles the next paragraph can play. Will it support an idea we've already been presented with? Will it focus on the other side of an argument? When your predictions are right, it's much easier to understand the next paragraph quickly. Even when your predictions are wrong, the act of anticipating something, and recognizing the text as being something else, will make you a stronger reader.

And finally, as you begin to read the next paragraph…

## Reassess

Take note when the passage unravels in a way you didn't expect. Constantly reassess your understanding as you read. Perhaps new information alters your perception of the central argument, or the author uses the argument as a springboard for a tangential discussion, or the author surprises you with an opinion you didn't expect.

Note that we recommend this PEAR process to everyone, no matter the notation process you use. An internal review process is a constant characteristic of all effective readers.

**4**

# DRILL IT: Annotation

Let's use the following passage to practice the annotation methods we've discussed. Annotate as you read the following passage by underlining and symbolizing, or by taking notes. Remember to go through the PEAR process as well. Give yourself four minutes. Afterwards, we'll discuss whether your annotation method was effective for you.

### December 1999, Section 3, Passage 2

**4**

Tragic dramas written in Greece during the fifth century B.C. engender considerable scholarly debate over the relative influence of individual autonomy and the power of the gods on the drama's action. One early scholar, B. Snell, argues that Aeschylus, for example, develops in his tragedies a concept of the autonomy of the individual. In these dramas, the protagonists invariably confront a situation that paralyzes them, so that their prior notions about how to behave or think are dissolved. Faced with a decision on which their fate depends, they must reexamine their deepest motives, and then act with determination. They are given only two alternatives, each with grave consequences, and they make the decision only after a tortured internal debate. According to Snell, this decision is "free" and "personal" and such personal autonomy constitutes the central theme in Aeschylean drama, as if the plays were devised to isolate an abstract model of human action. Drawing psychological conclusions from this interpretation, another scholar, Z. Barbu, suggests that "[Aeschylean] drama is proof of the emergence within ancient Greek civilization of the individual as a free agent."

To A. Rivier, Snell's emphasis on the decision made by the protagonist, with its implicit notions of autonomy and responsibility, misrepresents the role of the superhuman forces at work, forces that give the dramas their truly tragic dimension. These forces are not only external to the protagonist; they are also experienced by the protagonist as an internal compulsion, subjecting him or her to constraint even in what are claimed to be his or her "choices." Hence all that the deliberation does is to make the protagonist aware of the impasse, rather than motivating one choice over another. It is finally a necessity imposed by the deities that generates the decision, so that at a particular moment in the drama necessity dictates a path. Thus, the protagonist does not so much "choose" between two possibilities as "recognize" that there is only one real option.

A. Lesky, in his discussion of Aeschylus' play *Agamemnon*, disputes both views. Agamemnon, ruler of Argos, must decide whether to brutally sacrifice his own daughter. A message from the deity Artemis has told him that only the sacrifice will bring a wind to blow his ships to an important battle. Agamemnon is indeed constrained by a divine necessity. But he also deeply desires a victorious battle: "If this sacrifice will loose the winds, it is permitted to desire it fervently," he says. The violence of his passion suggest that Agamemnon chooses a path—chosen by the gods for their own reasons—on the basis of desires that must be condemned by us, because they are his own. In Lesky's view, tragic action is bound by the constant tension between a self and superhuman forces.

**MANHATTAN**
LSAT

# Was Your Method Effective?

In a moment, we'll break down how the annotation method *could* have played out relative to this passage, but let's pause for a moment to discuss the effectiveness of your own method.

In order to evaluate this, we don't need a "solution" to compare with. Everyone's process will be a little bit different, and the act of underlining one particular clause might have a different effect for you than it does for another reader.

When it comes to effective annotation, the proof is in the pudding: that is, **your method was effective for you if it helped you accomplish the correct goals**.

Review your annotation process now. If you underlined and marked up, reread only the underlined parts of the passage. If you took notes, only focus on those notes.

If your process was effective, it should help you:

1. Figure out the central argument.
2. Assign opinions to different sides.
3. Recognize the purpose of all supporting information.

If your notes *don't* help you accomplish any of these goals, or, worse yet, if your notes confuse you, then you know you need more practice, or a different system.

# SOLUTION: Annotation

This solution has three separate components:

    1. The passage is underlined and marked up.

    2. Notes on the passage are written in bold on the side (note you should have done 1 or 2, not both).

    3. The imagined PEAR process is contained in the boxes.

**4**

Tragic dramas written in Greece during the fifth century B.C. engender considerable scholarly debate over the relative influence of individual autonomy and the power of the gods on the drama's action. One early scholar, B. Snell, argues that Aeschylus, for example, develops in his tragedies a concept of the autonomy of the individual. In these dramas, the protagonists invariably confront a situation that paralyzes them, so that their prior notions about how to behave or think are dissolved. Faced with a decision on which their fate depends, they must reexamine their deepest motives, and then act with determination. They are given only two alternatives, each with grave consequences, and they make the decision only after a tortured internal debate. According to Snell, this decision is "free" and "personal" and such personal autonomy constitutes the central theme in Aeschylean drama, as if the plays were devised to isolate an abstract model of human action. Drawing psychological conclusions from this interpretation, another scholar, Z. Barbu, suggests that "[Aeschylean] drama is proof of the emergence within ancient Greek civilization of the individual as a free agent."

(1) *Individual autonomy drives Greek drama*
                *vs*
  *Power of gods drives Greek drama*

(2)

$O_1$ — *O for individual autonomy*

} *support for individual autonomy*

$O_1$ — *O for individual autonomy*

---

**Pause and Evaluate:**

*Gave us central argument: Greek drama driven by individual autonomy or power of gods. Rest of paragraph confirms understanding of central argument. Two opinions given for individual autonomy.*
**Anticipate:**
*More support for individual autonomy, or evidence for the other side.*

---

To A. Rivier, Snell's emphasis on the decision made by the protagonist, with its implicit notions of autonomy and responsibility, misrepresents the role of the superhuman forces at work, forces that give the dramas their truly tragic dimension. These forces are not only external to the protagonist; they are also experienced by the protagonist as an internal compulsion, subjecting him or her to constraint even in what are claimed to be his or her "choices." Hence all that the deliberation does is to make the protagonist aware of the impasse, rather than motivating one choice over another. It is finally a

$O_2$ — *O for power of gods*

} *support for power of gods*

**MANHATTAN**
LSAT

necessity imposed by the deities that generates the decision, so that at a particular moment in the drama necessity dictates a path. Thus, the protagonist does not so much "choose" between two possibilities as "recognize" that there is only one real option.

> *Pause and Evaluate:*
> *Evidence for power of the gods.*
>
> *Anticipate:*
> *More support for individual autonomy, or evidence for power of the gods.*

**4**

A. Lesky, in his discussion of Aeschylus' play Agamemnon, disputes both views. (O₃) Agamemnon, ruler of Argos, must decide whether to brutally sacrifice his own daughter. A message from the deity Artemis has told him that only the sacrifice will bring a wind to blow his ships to an important battle. Agamemnon is indeed constrained by a divine necessity. But he also deeply desires a victorious battle: "If this sacrifice will loose the winds, it is permitted to desire it fervently," he says. The violence of his passion suggest that Agamemnon chooses a path—chosen by the gods for their own reasons—on the basis of desires that must be condemned by us, because they are his own. In Lesky's view, tragic action is bound by the constant tension between a self and superhuman forces.

}

***different idea: Greek drama driven by conflict between both***

> *Reassess:*
> *New type of opinion: Disputes both views.*

> *Pause and Evaluate:*
> *Final view: Greek drama based on struggle between individual autonomy and power of gods.*

# Chapter 5

## *of*

## Reading Comprehension

### Part 2: *Master the Questions*

# The Search for

# Correct Answers

# Getting Familiar

Read the following passage and answer the questions to the best of your ability. For more rigorous practice, try to answer all the questions *without* looking back at the text. While even the best test-takers will refer back to the text at time, overreliance on rereading a passage can easily slow you down too much.

### *December 2003, Section 3, Passage 1*

Most of what has been written about Thurgood Marshall, a former United States Supreme Court justice who served from 1967 to 1991, has just focused
(5) on his judicial record and on the ideological content of his earlier achievements as a lawyer pursuing civil rights issues in the courts. But when Marshall's career is viewed from a technical perspective, his work with
(10) the NAACP (National Association for the Advancement of Colored People) reveals a strategic and methodical legacy to the field of public interest law. Though the NAACP, under Marshall's direction, was not the first
(15) legal organization in the U.S. to be driven by a political and social agenda, he and the NAACP developed innovations that forever changed the landscape of public interest law: during the 1940s and 1950s, in their
(20) campaign against state-sanctioned racial segregation, Marshall and the NAACP, instead of simply pursuing cases as the opportunity arose, set up a predetermined legal campaign that was meticulously crafted
(25) and carefully coordinated.

One aspect of this campaign, the test case strategy, involved sponsoring litigation of tactically chosen cases at the trial court level with careful evaluation of the precedential
(30) nuances and potential impact of each decision. This allowed Marshall to try out different approaches and discover which was the best to be used. An essential element in the success of this tactic was the explicit
(35) recognition that in a public interest legal campaign, choosing the right plaintiff can mean the difference between success and failure. Marshall carefully selected cases with sympathetic litigants, whose public
(40) appeal, credibility, and commitment to the

NAACP's goals were unsurpassed.

In addition, Marshall used sociological and psychological statistics—presented in expert testimony, for example, about
(45) the psychological impact of enforced segregation—as a means of transforming constitutional law by persuading the courts that certain discriminatory laws produced public harms in violation of constitutional
(50) principles. This tactic, while often effective, has been criticized by some legal scholars as a pragmatic attempt to give judges nonlegal material with which to fill gaps in their justifications for decisions where the purely
(55) legal principles appear inconclusive.

Since the time of Marshall's work with the NAACP, the number of public interest law firms in the U.S. has grown substantially, and they have widely adopted his
(60) combination of strategies for litigation, devoting them to various public purposes. These strategies have been used, for example, in consumer advocacy campaigns and, more recently, by politically conservative
(65) public interest lawyers seeking to achieve, through litigation, changes in the law that they have not been able to accomplish in the legislature. If we focus on the particular content of Marshall's goals and successes,
(70) it might seem surprising that his work has influenced the quest for such divergent political objects, but the techniques that he honed—originally considered to be a radical departure from accepted conventions —have
(75) become the norm for U.S. public interest litigation today.

## IDENTIFICATION

7. According to the passage, some legal scholars have criticized which of the following?

(A) the ideology Marshall used to support his goals

(B) recent public interest campaigns

(C) the use of Marshall's techniques by politically conservative lawyers

(D) the use of psychological statistics in court cases

(E) the set of criteria for selecting public interest litigants

## INFERENCE

5. The passage provides the most support for which one of the following statements?

(A) The ideological motivations for Marshall's work with the NAACP changed during his tenure on the U.S. Supreme Court.

(B) Marshall declined to pursue some cases that were in keeping with the NAACP's goals but whose plaintiffs' likely impression on the public he deemed to be unfavorable.

(C) Marshall's tactics were initially opposed by some other members of the NAACP who favored a more traditional approach.

(D) Marshall relied more on expert testimony in lower courts, whose judges were more likely than higher court judges to give weight to statistical evidence.

(E) Marshall's colleagues at the NAACP subsequently revised his methods and extended their applications to areas of law and politics beyond those for which they were designed.

## SYNTHESIS

1. Which one of the following most accurately expresses the main point of the passage?

(A) In his role as a lawyer for the NAACP, Marshall developed a number of strategies for litigation which, while often controversial, proved to be highly successful in arguing against certain discriminatory laws.

(B) The litigation strategies that Marshall devised in pursuit of the NAACP's civil rights goals during the 1940s and 1950s constituted significant innovations that have since been adopted as standard tactics for public interest lawyers.

(C) Although commentary on Marshall has often focused only on a single ideological aspect of his accomplishments, a reinvestigation of his record as a judge reveals its influence on current divergent political objectives.

(D) In his work with the NAACP during the 1940's and 1950's, Marshall adopted a set of tactics that were previously considered a radical departure from accepted practice, but which he adapted in such a way that they eventually became accepted conventions in the field of law.

(E) Contrary to the impression commonly given by commentary on Marshall, his contributions to the work of the NAACP have had more of a lasting impact than his achievements as a U.S. Supreme Court justice.

5

# The Search for Correct Answers

Okay, you've read the passage. You understand the argument, and you understand how everything else in the passage relates to that argument. Now what?

Now comes the important part. They don't give you points for reading. They give you points for answering questions correctly. And since you've gotten through the passage so quickly, you have the extra time you need to consider each question carefully. You're going to need it! Let's look at some challenges that the LSAT presents:

**1. The questions are often asked in a vague or confusing fashion.** Consider the prompt:

*"Critics of the author's argument would most likely disagree with which of the following?"*

Notice the double negative (critics, disagree). This is a complicated way of essentially asking you what the author would agree with.

**2. There is no direct correlation between prompt language and question type.** The test-taker has an advantage if he or she knows what type of answer to look out for. Unfortunately, there is often no direct correlation between prompt language and question type. Some questions give you a clear indication of what types of answers you are looking for, but some questions don't. Consider the vague prompt:

*"According to the passage, the author believes that…"*

The answer could be something general that relates to the whole passage, or it could be something specific, a detail mentioned in a supporting paragraph.

**3. The best answer is often not an ideal answer.** The best available answer choice is often incomplete, or worded in an unnecessarily challenging manner. This is especially true for higher level questions. The answer to a general question may not encompass all the main points made in a passage; the answer to a specific question may not be completely provable. Sometimes, an answer is correct simply because it is better than all the others that are presented.

Here's how we overcome these challenges:

**1. Read for a structural understanding of the passage relative to an argument.** Most questions are related in a direct or indirect manner to the roles that parts of the passage play with respect to a central argument. Reading and understanding the passage relative to the argument will allow you to correctly understand the function of its various parts. It also will allow you to more easily see connections between the evidence and opinions presented. This will give you intuitive advantages (for example, knowing the author's opinion relative to the argument often makes it much easier to spot obviously incorrect answer choices) and practical advantages (for example, having a structural understanding should help you locate pieces of text relevant to a specific question faster).

**2. Recognize the common characteristics of correct answers.** What skills is the LSAT testing exactly? The test-taker can have an advantage if he or she knows exactly what types of mental processes are tested and what types are not. We'll discuss this at length starting on the next page.

**3. Recognize the common characteristics of incorrect answer choices.** Imagine that the people who write the LSAT start off each question with five *correct* answer choices. One by one, they introduce flaws into four of the choices. What types of flaws do they introduce? What can you look out for that will tip you off to a wrong answer? As we mentioned above, right answers are often not ideal. The only way to get a high percentage of questions correct is to be able to confidently eliminate incorrect choices. We will discuss this at length in the next chapter.

**4. Use a consistent approach.** If you continuously read passages in a passive, aimless manner, and continuously choose answers based on vague, "gut feeling" sorts of reasons, you are asking way too much of your intuition! You may start out with a decent baseline score, because you may be a strong reader, but you are not making the test easier for yourself, and, most important, you are not giving yourself a real chance to improve. A systematic approach gives you a way to *organize* the various thought processes you must go through in order to successfully and accurately attack a question. Furthermore, a consistent process will help you *identify* your flaws and weaknesses more easily so that you can correct them. Use each chapter and each drill to hone your approach.

# The Characteristics of Correct Answers

We can generalize the skills that are tested on the LSAT Reading Comprehension test into three categories: identification, inference, and synthesis.

## Identification

Identification is the first level of understanding. About 1–2 questions per passage depend solely on your ability to identify and understand the meaning of a specific piece of text. These questions will tend to involve pieces of text that are difficult to find, and often involve answers that you might not expect. For Identification questions, *always* find "proof sentences" in the text to verify your answer choice.

## Inference

Inference questions ask you to go a step further. They ask you to identify a piece of text and then derive other truths from it. The correct answers to Inference questions require you to take a logical step that may be *unexpected*, but is nevertheless *valid*.

For example, if a piece of text states, "Most people prefer Brand X to Brand Y," we can infer:

1. Most people do not prefer Brand Y.
2. At least some people prefer Brand Y to Brand X.

If the passage states, "The census counted people in various occupational categories, including farming," we can infer:

1. Farming is an occupational category.
2. The census counted people in other occupations besides farming.

It is impossible to anticipate every inference. However, you should have a strong sense of what types of inferences are valid, and what types are not.

Going back to the first statement, "Most people prefer Brand X to Brand Y," it would be *incorrect* to infer:

1. Brand X is better than Brand Y (people don't always prefer the better product).
2. Brand X sells more than Brand Y (people don't always buy what they prefer; maybe Brand Y is cheaper).

Inference questions are the most common type you will see. Expect 2–5 Inference questions for every passage.

## Synthesis

Some questions require you to take one final step: once you've identified the relevant pieces of text and inferred correctly from them, you must synthesize these elements into some greater understanding.

For example, if we learn in the first paragraph that "critics don't like the plan because it is not cost-effective," and we learn in the third paragraph that "the few parents who support the plan represent a minority who disagree with the idea that the plan is bad for children," we can connect these two ideas and conclude that "critics and most parents share a common opinion, though their reasoning for that opinion may differ." Incorrect answers to Synthesis questions will often infer correctly from one piece of information but not the other, or they will combine ideas in an incorrect manner. Most Synthesis questions pertain to the passage as a whole, and a structural understanding of the passage relative to a central argument is a tremendous asset for answering these types of questions. Expect to see 1–4 Synthesis questions per passage.

## How These Skills Relate to One Another

In order to infer correctly, you must first identify the relevant piece of text. In order to synthesize, you must be able to identify and infer. Notice how these skills build upon one another.

**COMPREHENSION SKILLS**

| | | SYNTHESIS SKILLS |
| --- | --- | --- |
| | INFERENCE SKILLS | INFERENCE SKILLS |
| IDENTIFICATION SKILLS | IDENTIFICATION SKILLS | IDENTIFICATION SKILLS |

| IDENTIFICATION SKILLS | INFERENCE SKILLS | SYNTHESIS QUESTIONS |
| --- | --- | --- |

Of course, it is unnecessary to consciously think about this chart as you answer questions on the real test. However, understanding this chart should help you hone your sense of what a correct answer should accomplish. For example, if you've answered a Synthesis question correctly, you should be able to see that you first had to identify different parts of the passage and then infer from those parts. Likewise, if you answered an Inference question without first identifying the relevant piece of text, be suspicious of your answer.

Let's look back at our example in order to better understand each comprehension skill.

**5**

# Answers, Explanations, and Tips

First, let's be sure we've understood the passage. Here's our representation of the scale image:

### *December 2003, Section 3, Passage 1*

Most of what has been written about Thurgood Marshall, a former United States Supreme Court justice who served from 1967 to 1991, has just focused on his judicial record and on the ideological content of his
(5) earlier achievements as a lawyer pursuing civil rights issues in the courts. But when Marshall's career is viewed from a technical perspective, his work with the NAACP (National Association for the Advancement of Colored People) reveals a strategic and methodical
(10) legacy to the field of public interest law. Though the NAACP, under Marshall's direction, was not the first legal organization in the U.S. to be driven by a political and social agenda, he and the NAACP developed innovations that forever changed the landscape of
(15) public interest law: during the 1940s and 1950s, in their campaign against state-sanctioned racial segregation, Marshall and the NAACP, instead of simply pursuing cases as the opportunity arose, set up a predetermined legal campaign that was meticulously
(20) crafted and carefully coordinated.

One aspect of this campaign, the test case strategy, involved sponsoring litigation of tactically chosen cases at the trial court level with careful evaluation of the precedential nuances and potential impact of each
(25) decision. This allowed Marshall to try out different approaches and discover which was the best to be used. An essential element in the success of this tactic was the explicit recognition that in a public interest legal campaign, choosing the right plaintiff can mean the
(30) difference between success and failure. Marshall carefully selected cases with sympathetic litigants, whose public appeal, credibility, and commitment to the NAACP's goals were unsurpassed.

In addition, Marshall used sociological and
(35) psychological statistics—presented in expert testimony, for example, about the psychological impact of enforced segregation—as a means of transforming constitutional law by persuading the courts that certain discriminatory laws produced public harms in violation
(40) of constitutional principles. This tactic, while often effective, has been criticized by some legal scholars as a pragmatic attempt to give judges nonlegal material with which to fill gaps in their justifications for decisions where the purely legal principles appear inconclusive.

(45) Since the time of Marshall's work with the NAACP, the number of public interest law firms in the U.S. has grown substantially, and they have widely adopted his combination of strategies for litigation,
(50) devoting them to various public purposes. These strategies have been used, for example, in consumer advocacy campaigns and, more recently, by politically conservative public interest lawyers seeking to achieve, through litigation, changes in the law that they have not
(55) been able to accomplish in the legislature. If we focus on the particular content of Marshall's goals and successes, it might seem surprising that his work has influenced the quest for such divergent political objects, but the techniques that he honed—
(60) originally considered to be a radical departure from accepted conventions —have become the norm for U.S. public interest litigation today.

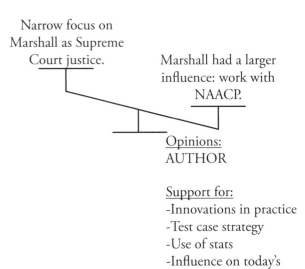

Narrow focus on Marshall as Supreme Court justice.

Marshall had a larger influence: work with NAACP.

Opinions:
AUTHOR

Support for:
-Innovations in practice
-Test case strategy
-Use of stats
-Influence on today's public interest litigation

*Note that the argument, developed at the start of the passage, is used as a springboard to discuss the specifics of Marshall's work with the NAACP. The argument isn't the central focus here, but it helps us to organize the information that comes later.*

## IDENTIFICATION

7. According to the passage, some legal scholars have criticized which of the following?

(A)  the ideology Marshall used to support his goals

(B)  recent public interest campaigns

(C)  the use of Marshall's techniques by politically conservative lawyers

(D)  the use of psychological statistics in court cases

(E)  the set of criteria for selecting public interest litigants

### Referenced text:

In addition, Marshall used sociological and
(35) psychological statistics—presented in expert testimony, for example, about the psychological impact of enforced segregation—as a means of transforming constitutional law by persuading the courts that certain discriminatory laws produced public harms in violation
(40) of constitutional principles. **This tactic**, while often effective, has been criticized by some legal scholars...

**Comment:**

*Notice that the right answer here requires very little interpretation. It is easy to overthink Identification questions. Just look for an answer that provides a good match between material in the question and material in the text. Here we want to look for material that matches "legal scholars have criticized." We can find this in the third paragraph. A good general understanding from your first read should make it easier to find the relevant piece of text quickly. In other words, the better you have the passage organized, the easier your search will be.*

*The LSAT has tried to make this question more difficult by using the relative phrase "this tactic" in the text (bolded to the left). It requires a little extra work to confirm that "this tactic" refers to the use of sociological and psychological statistics.*

*The other answers are mentioned in the text, and it's not unreasonable to think that some of them can or should be criticized. However, the only one that is clearly stated as having been specifically criticized is (D).*

## Tips for Identification Questions

**1. Look for "identification" cues.** Use the question stem *and* the answer choices as clues to help you recognize the question type. Here, "according to the passage" tips us off that it is probably identification instead of inference, and "legal scholars" and "criticized" narrow our scope. Furthermore, every item in the answer list is something that is explicitly mentioned in (rather than inferred from) the passage. Together, all these clues tell us that the question probably just requires simple identification.

**2. Watch out for false matches.** Don't pick an answer just because you vaguely remember reading something similar in the text. Confirm that the text does match up specifically with the particular question stem and answer choice. In this question, the other answers are mentioned in the text, but they are not specifically what the legal scholars have criticized.

**3. Connect with the text.** If you are stuck, don't spend extra time comparing answers against one another. Instead, spend that time rereading the passage to locate the relevant text. Nothing in the answer choices in and of themselves will tip you off. It's only by connecting the choices with the text that you can confirm your answer.

**INFERENCE**

5. The passage provides the most support for which one of the following statements?

(A) The ideological motivations for Marshall's work with the NAACP changed during his tenure on the U.S. Supreme Court.

(B) Marshall declined to pursue some cases that were in keeping with the NAACP's goals but whose plaintiffs' likely impression on the public he deemed to be unfavorable.

(C) Marshall's tactics were initially opposed by some other members of the NAACP who favored a more traditional approach.

(D) Marshall relied more on expert testimony in lower courts, whose judges were more likely than higher court judges to give weight to statistical evidence.

(E) Marshall's colleagues at the NAACP subsequently revised his methods and extended their applications to areas of law and politics beyond those for which they were designed.

**Comment:**

*The phrase "most support" tips us off that we may be looking to do something more than just identify. We need to use something in the text to prove something else. Though this is an Inference question, the process of answering is similar—we want to start by identifying the relevant part of the text. Again, a good first read gives us a solid understanding of the organization of the passage. If we've done a good job of constructing the scale image, perhaps we remember that the test case strategy was the first innovation mentioned; this in turn helps us to speed up our search for this text in the passage.*

*(A) is simply not mentioned in the text. (C), (D) and (E) stray too far from what we've been given. If we know that Marshall screened cases to find sympathetic litigants, we can logically deduce that he declined some cases involving unsympathetic litigants.*

**Referenced text:**

...can mean the
(30) difference between success and failure. Marshall carefully selected cases with sympathetic litigants, whose public appeal, credibility, and commitment to the NAACP's goals were unsurpassed.

## Tips for Inference Questions

**1. Identify before you infer.** Infer only after you've found the relevant part of the text. It will make your work much easier!

**2. Eliminate attractive wrong answers by comparing them to specific, relevant parts of text.** Obviously, you don't have time to double-check every answer choice, but you do want to confirm or deny the most attractive answers by comparing them against the relevant parts of the text. Here, (C) is an attractive answer. It's easy to get the impression that others in the NAACP were initially opposed to Marshall's tactics (because these tactics were new and innovative), but that is never directly or indirectly supported by the text. (E) is also attractive. It's easy to misread the end and assume that the NAACP extended his work into other areas, but a rereading of the last paragraph confirms that there is no support for this inference. Someone used Marshall's tactics for other purposes, but not necessarily the NAACP.

**3. Don't infer too much!** Many of the wrong choices sound attractive because they are (1) reasonable, and (2) in some indirect way connected to the text. Right answers to Inference questions need to be more than that—they should be fairly provable using the text. Resist answers that require illogical leaps or logical ones that are too big.

MANHATTAN
LSAT

**SYNTHESIS**

1. Which one of the following most accurately expresses the main point of the passage?

(A) In his role as a lawyer for the NAACP, Marshall developed a number of strategies for litigation which, while often controversial, proved to be highly successful in arguing against certain discriminatory laws.

(B) The litigation strategies that Marshall devised in pursuit of the NAACP's civil rights goals during the 1940s and 1950s constituted significant innovations that have since been adopted as standard tactics for public interest lawyers.

(C) Although commentary on Marshall has often focused only on a single ideological aspect of his accomplishments, a reinvestigation of his record as a judge reveals its influence on current divergent political objectives.

(D) In his work with the NAACP during the 1940's and 1950's, Marshall adopted a set of tactics that were previously considered a radical departure from accepted practice, but which he adapted in such a way that they eventually became accepted conventions in the field of law.

(E) Contrary to the impression commonly given by commentary on Marshall, his contributions to the work of the NAACP have had more of a lasting impact than his achievements as a U.S. Supreme Court justice.

**Referenced text:**

But when Marshall's career is
viewed from a technical perspective, his work with the
NAACP (National Association for the Advancement of
Colored People) reveals a strategic and methodical
(10) legacy to the field of public interest law…

…and social agenda, he and the NAACP developed
innovations that forever changed the landscape of
(15) public interest law…

…such divergent political
objects, but the techniques that he honed—
(60) originally considered to be a radical departure from
accepted conventions—have become the norm for U.S.
public interest litigation today.

**Comment:**

*Synthesis questions often test your understanding of the passage as a whole (or parts of the passage relative to the whole), but what often makes Synthesis questions challenging is that correct and incorrect answers often hinge on subtle, small details. If you read in a casual fashion, several of these answers seem similar to one another and many seem correct.*

*Answer choice (B) is the best available because it is the only one without a marked flaw. (A) speaks to the "success" of the strategies; though "success" is mentioned in the passage, this answer choice fails to note the transformative impact that Marshall had on public interest litigation. Thus, while (A) is a provable statement, its scope is too narrow to accurately express the main point of the passage. (C) incorrectly focuses on his experiences as a judge, whereas the bulk of the passage is about his work with the NAACP. A good understanding of the scale will help us eliminate (C). Remember, the argument (Marshal as judge vs. Marshall with NAACP) is just a springboard to get to the main content of the passage: the details of his work with the NAACP. (D) is very attractive, but incorrect in small degrees. He did not adapt the tactics, he invented them ("developed innovations"). And the passage does not talk about his tactics becoming accepted conventions for the entire field of law, but rather for the niche of public interest work. (E) captures the essence of the argument that we noted in our scale, but the argument is not of central importance here and does not capture the "main point" of the passage. Rather, it's used as a springboard. Besides, (E) goes too far in claiming that one part of his life was more significant than the other; the passage itself does not make such a bold claim.*

*Note that answer (B) does a good job of synthesizing multiple pieces of the text.*

## Tips for Synthesis Questions

**1. Be flexible.** Understanding the argument structure is key, but so is flexibility. Remember, the correct answer is often not an ideal one, and it's often different from the answer you might predict. Sometimes the right answer does a poor job of summarizing the passage as a whole. Keep an open mind, and eliminate only those choices that you are certain are incorrect.

**2. See the forest *and* the trees.** Yes, these questions are primarily about general understanding, but right and wrong answers are often determined by subtle details. If two or three different answers seem the same to you, look for small differences in the wording between them and compare these differences against the text.

**3. Use the author's opinion as the tipping point.** Incorrect choices often misrepresent the author's opinion, both in terms of what side of the argument it falls on and how subtle or strong that opinion is. A correct understanding of the author's opinion will often help you pick the correct answer.

**4. Watch out for "narrow scope" answers.** We'll soon discuss the characteristics of incorrect answers. For now, know that many incorrect answers to Synthesis questions are actually true in terms of their content (e.g., answer choice (A) on the previous question), but too narrow in scope to accurately express the main point of the passage.

**5**

*Page left intentionally blank.*

5

# DRILL IT: Correct Answer Characteristics

Each of the following passages has four questions attached; these questions are all Identification, Inference, or Synthesis questions. Give yourself six minutes per passage to read the text and answer all the questions. After you review the correct answers, use the tracking chart to determine your comfort level with the different question types.

### December 2003, Section 3, Passage 3

Because the market system enables entrepreneurs and investors who develop new technology to reap financial rewards from their risk of capital, it may seem that the primary result of this activity is that some
(5) people who have spare capital accumulate more. But in spite of the fact that the profits derived from various technological developments have accrued to relatively few people, the developments themselves have served overall as a remarkable democratizing force. In fact,
(10) under the regime of the market, the gap in benefits accruing to different groups of people has been narrowed in the long term.

This tendency can be seen in various well-known technological developments. For example, before the
(15) printing press was introduced centuries ago, few people had access to written materials, much less to scribes and private secretaries to produce and transcribe documents. Since printed materials have become widely available, however, people without special
(20) position or resources—and in numbers once thought impossible—can take literacy and the use of printed texts for granted. With the distribution of books and periodicals in public libraries, this process has been extended to the point where people in general can have
(25) essentially equal access to a vast range of texts that would once have been available only to a very few. A more recent technological development extends this process beyond printed documents. A child in school access to a personal computer and modem—
(30) which is becoming fairly common in technologically advanced societies—has computing power and database access equal to that of the best-connected scientists and engineers at top-level labs of just fifteen years ago, a time when relatively few people had
(35) personal access to any computing power. Or consider the uses of technology for leisure. In previous centuries only a few people with abundant resources had the ability and time to hire professional entertainment, and to have contact through travel and written
(40) communication—both of which were prohibitively expensive—with distant people. But now broadcast technology is widely available, and so almost anyone can have an entertainment cornucopia unimagined in earlier times. Similarly, the development of

(45) inexpensive mail distribution and telephone connection and, more recently, the establishment of the even more efficient medium of electronic mail have greatly extended the power of distant communication.

This kind of gradual diffusion of benefits across
(50) society is not an accident of these particular technological developments, but rather the result of a general tendency of the market system. Entrepreneurs and investors often are unable to maximize financial success without expanding their market, and this
(55) involves structuring their prices to the consumers so as to make their technologies genuinely accessible to an ever-larger share of the population. In other words, because market competition drives prices down, it tends to diffuse access to new technology across society as a result.

16. Which one of the following does the passage identify as being a result of technological development?

(A) burgeoning scientific research
(B) educational uses of broadcasting
(C) widespread exchange of political ideas
(D) faster means of travel
(E) increased access to databases

18. Which one of the following most accurately represents the primary function of the reference to maximization of financial success (lines 52–54)?

(A) It forms part of the author's summary of the benefits that have resulted from the technological developments described in the preceding paragraph.
(B) It serves as the author's logical conclusion from data presented in the preceding paragraph regarding the social consequences of technological development.
(C) It forms part of a speculative hypothesis that the author presents for its interest in relation to the main topic rather than as part of an argument.
(D) It serves as part of a causal explanation that reinforces the thesis in the first paragraph regarding the benefits of technological development.
(E) It forms part of the author's concession that certain factors complicate the argument presented in the first two paragraphs.

19. It can be most reasonably inferred from the passage that the author would agree with which one of the following statements?

(A) The profits derived from computer technology have accrued to fewer people than have the profits derived from any other technological development.
(B) Often the desire of some people for profits motivates changes that are beneficial for large numbers of other people.
(C) National boundaries are rarely barriers to the democratizing spread of technology.
(D) Typically, investment in technology is riskier than many other sorts of investment.
(E) Greater geographical mobility of populations has contributed to the profits of entrepreneurs and investors in technology.

20. From the passage it can be most reasonably inferred that the author would agree with which one of the following statements?

(A) The democratizing influence of technology generally contributes to technological obsolescence.
(B) Wholly unregulated economies are probably the fastest in producing an equalization of social status.
(C) Expanded access to printed texts across a population has historically led to an increase in literacy in that population.
(D) The invention of the telephone has had a greater democratizing influence on society than has the invention of the printing press.
(E) Near equality of financial assets among people is a realistic goal for market economies.

### December 2003, Section 3, Passage 4

Neurobiologists once believed that the workings of the brain were guided exclusively by electrical signals; according to this theory, communication between neurons (brain cells) is possible because electrical
(5) impulses travel from one neuron to the next by literally leaping across synapses (gaps between neurons). But many neurobiologists puzzled over how this leaping across synapses might be achieved, and as early as 1904 some speculated that electrical impulses
(10) are transmitted between neurons chemically rather than electrically. According to this alternative theory, the excited neuron secretes a chemical called a neurotransmitter that binds with its corresponding receptor molecule in the receiving neuron. This binding
(15) of the neurotransmitter renders the neuron permeable to ions, and as the ions move into the receiving neuron they generate an electrical impulse that runs through the cell; the electrical impulse is thereby transmitted to the receiving neuron.
(20)     This theory has gradually won acceptance in the scientific community, but for a long time little was known about the mechanism by which neurotransmitters manage to render the receiving neuron permeable to ions. In fact, some scientists
(25) remained skeptical of the theory because they had trouble imagining how the binding of a chemical to a receptor at the cell surface could influence the flow of ions through the cell membrane. Recently, however, researchers have gathered enough evidence for a
(30) convincing explanation: that the structure of receptors plays the pivotal role in mediating the conversion of chemical signals into electrical activity.

The new evidence shows that receptors for neurotransmitters contain both a neurotransmitter
(35) binding site and a separate region that functions as a channel for ions; attachment of the neurotransmitter to the binding site causes the receptor to change shape and so results in the opening of its channel component. Several types of receptors have been isolated that
(40) conform to this structure, among them the receptors for acetylcholine, gamma-aminobutyric acid (GABA), glycine, and serotonin. These receptors display enough similarities to constitute a family, known collectively as neurotransmitter-gated ion channels.
(45)     It has also been discovered that each of the receptors in this family comes in several varieties so that, for example, a GABA receptor in one part of the brain has slightly different properties than a GABA receptor in another part of the brain. This discovery is
(50) medically significant because it raises the possibility of the highly selective treatment of certain brain disorders. As the precise effect on behavior of every variety of each neurotransmitter-gated ion channel is deciphered, pharmacologists may be able to design
(55) drugs targeted to specific receptors on defined categories of neurons that will selectively impede or enhance these effects. Such drugs could potentially help ameliorate any number of debilitating conditions, including mood disorders, tissue damage associated
(60) with stroke, or Alzheimer's disease.

21. Which one of the following most completely and accurately states the main point of the passage?

(A) Evidence shows that the workings of the brain are guided, not by electrical signals, but by chemicals, and that subtle differences among the receptors for these chemicals may permit the selective treatment of certain brain disorders.

(B) Evidence shows that the workings of the brain are guided, not by electrical signals, but by chemicals, and that enough similarities exist among these chemicals to allow scientists to classify them as a family.

(C) Evidence shows that electrical impulses are transmitted between neurons chemically rather than electrically, and that enough similarities exist among these chemicals to allow scientists to classify them as a family.

(D) Evidence shows that electrical impulses are transmitted between neurons chemically rather than electrically, and that subtle differences among the receptors for these chemicals may permit the selective treatment of certain brain disorders.

(E) Evidence shows that receptor molecules in the brain differ subtly from one another, and that these differences can be exploited to treat certain brain disorders through the use of drugs that selectively affect particular parts of the brain.

23. Each of the following statements is affirmed by the passage EXCEPT:

(A) The secretion of certain chemicals plays a role in neuron communication.

(B) The flow of ions through neurons plays a role in neuron communication.

(C) The binding of neurotransmitters to receptors plays a role in neuron communication.

(D) The structure of receptors on neuron surfaces plays a role in neuron communication.

(E) The size of neurotransmitter binding sites on receptors plays a role in neuron communication.

24. The author most likely uses the phrase "defined categories of neurons" in lines 55–56 in order to refer to neurons that

(A) possess channels for ions
(B) respond to drug treatment
(C) contain receptor molecules
(D) influence particular brain functions
(E) react to binding by neurotransmitters

25. Which one of the following most accurately describes the organization of the passage?

(A) explanation of a theory; presentation of evidence in support of the theory; presentation of evidence in opposition to the theory; argument in favor of rejecting the theory; discussion of the implication of rejecting the theory

(B) explanation of a theory; presentation of evidence in support of the theory; explanation of an alternative theory; presentation of information to support the alternative theory; discussion of an experiment that can help determine which theory is correct

(C) explanation of a theory; description of an obstacle to the theory's general acceptance; presentation of an explanation that helps the theory overcome the obstacle; discussion of a further implication of the theory

(D) explanation of a theory; description of an obstacle to the theory's general acceptance; argument that the obstacle is insurmountable and that the theory should be rejected; discussion of the implications of rejecting the theory

(E) explanation of a theory; description of how the theory came to win scientific acceptance; presentation of new information that challenges the theory; modification of the theory to accommodate the new information; discussion of an implication of the modification.

### October 2003, Section 4, Passage 2

Countee Cullen (Countee Leroy Porter, 1903–1946) was one of the foremost poets of the Harlem Renaissance, the movement of African American writers, musicians, and artists centered in the
(5) Harlem section of New York City during the 1920's. Beginning with his university years, Cullen strove to establish himself as an author of romantic poetry on abstract, universal topics such as love and death. Believing poetry should consist of "lofty thoughts
(10) beautifully expressed," Cullen preferred controlled poetic forms. He used European forms such as sonnets and devices such as quatrains, couplets, and conventional rhyme, and he frequently employed classical allusions and Christian religious imagery,
(15) which were most likely the product both of his university education and of his upbringing as the adopted son of a Methodist Episcopal reverend.
   Some literary critics have praised Cullen's skill at writing European-style verse, finding, for example, in
(20) "The Ballad of the Brown Girl" an artful use of diction and a rhythm and sonority that allow him to capture the atmosphere typical of the English ballad form of past centuries. Others have found Cullen's use of European verse forms and techniques unsuited to treating
(25) political or racial themes, such as the themes in "Uncle Jim," in which a young man is told by his uncle of the different experiences of African Americans and whites in United States society, or "Incident," which relates the experience of an eight-year-old child who hears a racial
(30) slur. One such critic complained that Cullen's persona as expressed in his work sometimes seems to vacillate between aesthete and spokesperson for racial issues. But Cullen himself rejected this dichotomy, maintaining that his interest in romantic
(35) poetry was quite compatible with his concern over racial issues. He drew a distinction between poetry of solely political intent and his own work, which he believed reflected his identify as an African American. As the heartfelt expression of his personality
(40) accomplished by means of careful attention to his chosen craft, his work could not help but do so.
   Explicit references to racial matters do in fact decline in Cullen's later work, but not because he felt any less passionately about these matters. Rather,
(45) Cullen increasingly focused on the religious dimension of his poetry. In "The Black Christ," in which the poet imagines the death and resurrection of a rural African American, and "Heritage," which expresses the tension between the poet's identification with Christian
(50) traditions and his desire to stay close to his African heritage, Cullen's thoughts on race were subsumed within what he conceived of as broader and more urgent questions about the suffering and redemption of the soul. Nonetheless, Cullen never abandoned his
(55) commitment to the importance of racial issues, reflecting on one occasion that he felt "actuated by a strong sense of race consciousness" that "grows upon me, I find, as I grow older."

7. Which one of the following most accurately states the main point of the passage?

(A) While much of Cullen's poetry deals with racial issues, in his later work he became less concerned with racial matters and increasingly interested in writing poetry with a religious dimension.

(B) While Cullen used European verse forms and his later poems increasingly addressed religious themes, his poetry never abandoned a concern for racial issues.

(C) Though Cullen used European verse forms, he acknowledged that these forms were not very well suited to treating political or racial themes.

(D) Despite the success of Cullen's poetry at dealing with racial issues, Cullen's primary goal was to re-create the atmosphere that characterized the English ballad.

(E) The religious dimension throughout Cullen's poetry complemented his focus on racial issues by providing the context within which these issues could be understood.

8. Given the information in the passage, which one of the following most closely exemplifies Cullen's conception of poetry?

(A) a sonnet written with careful attention to the conventions of the form to re-create the atmosphere of sixteenth-century English poetry

(B) a sonnet written with deliberate disregard for the conventions of the form to illustrate the perils of political change

(C) a sonnet written to explore the aesthetic impact of radical innovations in diction, rhythm, and sonority

(D) a sonnet written with great stylistic freedom to express the emotional upheaval associated with romantic love

(E) a sonnet written with careful attention to the conventions of the form expressing feelings about the inevitability of death

9. Which one of the following is NOT identified by the author of the passage as characteristic of Cullen's poetry?

(A) It often deals with abstract, universal subject matter.

(B) It often employs rhyme, classical allusions, and religious imagery.

(C) It avoids traditional poetic forms in favor of formal experimentation.

(D) It sometimes deals explicitly with racial issues.

(E) It eventually subsumed racial issues into a discussion of religious issues.

10. The passage suggests which one of the following about Cullen's use of controlled poetic forms?

(A) Cullen used controlled poetic forms because he believed they provided the best means to beautiful poetic expression.

(B) Cullen's interest in religious themes naturally led him to use controlled poetic forms.

(C) Only the most controlled poetic forms allowed Cullen to address racial issues in his poems.

(D) Cullen had rejected the less controlled poetic forms he was exposed to prior to his university years.

(E) Less controlled poetic forms are better suited to poetry that addresses racial or political issues.

### October 2003, Section 4, Passage 4

Although philanthropy—the volunteering of private resources for humanitarian purposes—reached its apex in England in the late nineteenth century, modern commentators have articulated two major
(5) criticisms of the philanthropy that was a mainstay of England's middle-class Victorian society. The earlier criticism is that such philanthropy was even by the later nineteenth century obsolete, since industrialism had already created social problems that were beyond the
(10) scope of small, private voluntary efforts. Indeed, these problems required substantial legislative action by the state. Unemployment, for example, was not the result of a failure of diligence on the part of workers or a failure of compassion on the part of employers, nor
(15) could it be solved by well-wishing philanthropists.

The more recent charge holds that Victorian philanthropy was by its very nature a self-serving exercise carried out by philanthropists at the expense of those whom they were ostensibly serving. In this view,
(20) philanthropy was a means of flaunting one's power and position in a society that placed great emphasis on status, or even a means of cultivating social connections that could lead to economic rewards. Further, if philanthropy is seen as serving the interests
(25) of individual philanthropists, so it may be seen as serving the interests of their class. According to this "social control" thesis, philanthropists, in professing to help the poor, were encouraging in them such values as prudence, thrift, and temperance, values perhaps
(30) worthy in themselves but also designed to create more productive members of the labor force. Philanthropy, in short, was a means of controlling the labor force and ensuring the continued dominance of the management class.

(35) Modern critics of Victorian philanthropy often use the words "amateurish" or "inadequate" to describe Victorian philanthropy, as though Victorian charity can only be understood as an antecedent to the era of state-sponsored, professionally administered charity. This
(40) assumption is typical of the "Whig fallacy": the tendency to read the past as an inferior prelude to an enlightened present. If most Victorians resisted state control and expended their resources on private, voluntary philanthropies, it could only be, the argument
(45) goes, because of their commitment to a vested interest, or because the administrative apparatus of the state was incapable of coping with the economic and social needs of the time.

This version of history patronizes the Victorians,
(50) who were in fact well aware of their vulnerability to charges of condescension and complacency, but were equally well aware of the potential dangers of state-managed charity. They were perhaps condescending to the poor, but—to use an un-Victorian metaphor—they
(55) put their money where their mouths were, and gave of their careers and lives as well.

21. Which one of the following best summarizes the main idea of the passage?

(A) While the motives of individual practitioners have been questioned by modern commentators, Victorian philanthropy successfully dealt with the social ills of nineteenth-century England.

(B) Philanthropy, inadequate to deal with the massive social and economic problems of the twentieth century, has slowly been replaced by state-sponsored charity.

(C) The practice of reading the past as a prelude to an enlightened present has fostered revisionist views of many institutions, among them Victorian philanthropy.

(D) Although modern commentators have perceived Victorian philanthropy as either inadequate or self-serving, the theoretical bias behind these criticisms leads to an incorrect interpretation of history.

(E) Victorian philanthropists, aware of public resentment of their self-congratulatory attitude, used devious methods to camouflage their self serving motives.


22. According to the passage, which one of the following is true of both modern criticisms made about Victorian philanthropy?

(A) Both criticisms attribute dishonorable motives to those privileged individuals who engaged in private philanthropy.

(B) Both criticisms presuppose that the social rewards of charitable activity outweighed the economic benefits.

(C) Both criticisms underemphasize the complacency and condescension demonstrated by the Victorians.

(D) Both criticisms suggest that government involvement was necessary to cure social ills.

(E) Both criticisms take for granted the futility of efforts by private individuals to enhance their social status by means of philanthropy.


25. It can be inferred from the passage that a social control theorist would be most likely to agree with which one of the following statements concerning the motives of Victorian philanthropists?

(A) Victorian philanthropists were driven more by the desire for high social status than by the hope of economic gain.

(B) Victorian philanthropists encouraged such values as thrift and temperance in order to instill in the working class the same acquisitiveness that characterized the management class.

(C) Though basically well-intentioned, Victorian philanthropists faced problems that were far beyond the scope of private charitable organizations.

(D) By raising the living standards of the poor, Victorian philanthropists also sought to improve the intellectual status of the poor.

(E) Victorian philanthropists see philanthropy as a means to an end rather than as an end in itself.


26. Which of the following best describes the organization of the passage?

(A) Two related positions are discussed, then both are subjected to the same criticism.

(B) Two opposing theories are outlined, then a synthesis between the two is proposed.

(C) A position is stated, and two differing evaluations of it are given.

(D) Three examples of the same logical inconsistency are given.

(E) A theory is outlined, and two supporting examples are given.

# SOLUTIONS: Correct Answer Characteristics

**5**

### *December 2003, Section 3, Passage 3*

Because the market system enables entrepreneurs and investors who develop new technology to reap financial rewards from their risk of capital, it may seem that the primary result of this activity is that some
(5) people who have spare capital accumulate more. But in spite of the fact that the profits derived from various technological developments have accrued to relatively few people, the developments themselves have served overall as a remarkable democratizing force. In fact,
(10) under the regime of the market, the gap in benefits accruing to different groups of people has been narrowed in the long term.

This tendency can be seen in various well-known technological developments. For example, before the
(15) printing press was introduced centuries ago, few people had access to written materials, much less to scribes and private secretaries to produce and transcribe documents. Since printed materials have become widely available, however, people without special
(20) position or resources—and in numbers once thought impossible—can take literacy and the use of printed texts for granted. With the distribution of books and periodicals in public libraries, this process has been extended to the point where people in general can have
(25) essentially equal access to a vast range of texts that would once have been available only to a very few. A more recent technological development extends this process beyond printed documents. A child in school access to a personal computer and modem—
(30) which is becoming fairly common in technologically advanced societies—has computing power and database access equal to that of the best-connected scientists and engineers at top-level labs of just fifteen years ago, a time when relatively few people had
(35) personal access to any computing power. Or consider the uses of technology for leisure. In previous centuries only a few people with abundant resources had the ability and time to hire professional entertainment, and to have contact through travel and written
(40) communication—both of which were prohibitively expensive—with distant people. But now broadcast technology is widely available, and so almost anyone can have an entertainment cornucopia unimagined in earlier times. Similarly, the development of

(45) inexpensive mail distribution and telephone connection and, more recently, the establishment of the even more efficient medium of electronic mail have greatly extended the power of distant communication.

This kind of gradual diffusion of benefits across
(50) society is not an accident of these particular technological developments, but rather the result of a general tendency of the market system. Entrepreneurs and investors often are unable to maximize financial success without expanding their market, and this
(55) involves structuring their prices to the consumers so as to make their technologies genuinely accessible to an ever-larger share of the population. In other words, because market competition drives prices down, it tends to diffuse access to new technology across society as a result.

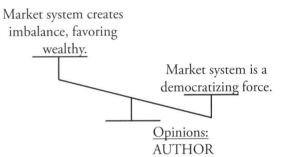

Market system creates imbalance, favoring wealthy.

Market system is a democratizing force.

Opinions: AUTHOR

Support for:
- Printing press
- Personal computer
- Broadcast technology
- Mail/phone/email
- Prices down, access up

*The argument is introduced right at the beginning of the passage; the remainder of the passage is used to provide examples and support for the author's opinion.*

## IDENTIFICATION

16. Which one of the following does the passage identify as being a result of technological development?

(A) burgeoning scientific research
(B) educational uses of broadcasting
(C) widespread exchange of political ideas
(D) faster means of travel
(E) increased access to databases

**Referenced text:**

…process beyond printed documents. A child in school with access to a personal computer and modem—
(30) which is becoming fairly common in technologically advanced societies—has computing power and database access equal to that of the best-connected scientists and engineers at top-level labs of just fifteen years ago, a time when relatively few people had
(35) personal access to any computing power.

**Comment:**

*The other answer choices seem like reasonable, logical results of technological development, but only answer choice (E) is specifically mentioned. Be careful not to overthink Identification questions. A general answer like (A) can seem attractive, but is hard to prove. Answer (D) is also attractive because "travel" is mentioned in line 41. However, "faster" travel is never discussed. Watch out for false matches!*

## SYNTHESIS

18. Which one of the following most accurately represents the primary function of the reference to maximization of financial success (lines 56–58)?

(A) It forms part of the author's summary of the benefits that have resulted from the technological developments described in the preceding paragraph.
(B) It serves as the author's logical conclusion from data presented in the preceding paragraph regarding the social consequences of technological development.
(C) It forms part of a speculative hypothesis that the author presents for its interest in relation to the main topic rather than as part of an argument.
(D) It serves as part of a causal explanation that reinforces the thesis in the first paragraph regarding the benefits of technological development.
(E) It forms part of the author's concession that certain factors complicate the argument presented in the first two paragraphs.

**Referenced text:**

(5) …people who have spare capital accumulate more. But in spite of the fact that the profits derived from various technological developments have accrued to relatively few people, the developments themselves have served overall as a remarkable democratizing force. In fact, under the regime of the market, the gap in benefits
(10) accruing to different groups of people has been narrowed in the long term.

…general tendency of the market system. Entrepreneurs and investors often are unable to
(55) maximize financial success without expanding their market, and this involves structuring their prices to the consumers so as to make their technologies genuinely accessible to an ever-larger share of the population…

**Comment:**

*The thesis in the first paragraph states that technological advancements are a democratizing force that has a positive impact on the general public, not just on the specific individuals who are responsible for the innovations. Did your scale help you understand this? Though this may seem like an Inference question, getting the correct answer requires a synthesis of information from more than one part of the passage.*

5

**INFERENCE**

19. It can be most reasonably inferred from the passage that the author would agree with which one of the following statements?

(A) The profits derived from computer technology have accrued to fewer people than have the profits derived from any other technological development.

(B) Often the desire of some people for profits motivates changes that are beneficial for large numbers of other people.

(C) National boundaries are rarely barriers to the democratizing spread of technology.

(D) Typically, investment in technology is riskier than many other sorts of investment.

(E) Greater geographical mobility of populations has contributed to the profits of entrepreneurs and investors in technology.

**Referenced text:**

Because the market system enables entrepreneurs and investors who develop new technology to reap financial rewards from their risk of capital, it may seem that the primary result of this activity is that some
(5) people who have spare capital accumulate more. But in spite of the fact that the profits derived from various technological developments have accrued to relatively few people, the developments themselves have served overall as a remarkable democratizing force.

...general tendency of the market system. Entrepreneurs and investors often are unable to
(55) maximize financial success without expanding their market, and this involves structuring their prices to the consumers so as to make their technologies genuinely accessible to an ever-larger share of the population...

**Comment:**

*Note that this inference requires no further assumptions or extrapolations on our part. The two portions of referenced text basically prove answer choice (B). Also, did you notice that answer (B) is essentially the right side of our scale?*

*All the other answer choices infer too much. If you need to add too many of your own assumptions to validate the answer to an Inference question, that answer is probably incorrect.*

**INFERENCE**

20. From the passage it can be most reasonably inferred that the author would agree with which one of the following statements?

(A) The democratizing influence of technology generally contributes to technological obsolescence.

(B) Wholly unregulated economies are probably the fastest in producing an equalization of social status.

(C) Expanded access to printed texts across a population has historically led to an increase in literacy in that population.

(D) The invention of the telephone has had a greater democratizing influence on society than has the invention of the printing press.

(E) Near equality of financial assets among people is a realistic goal for market economies.

**Referenced text:**

...documents. Since printed materials have become widely available, however, people without special
(20) position or resources—and in numbers once thought impossible—can take literacy and the use of printed texts for granted...

**Comment:**

*Again, the referenced text basically proves answer (C). If the expanded access has allowed us to take literacy for granted, we can infer that that access led to an increase in literacy.*

*The rest of the choices infer too much or require an added assumption or extrapolation. They simply cannot be proved using the information in the passage.*

MANHATTAN
LSAT

*December 2003, Section 3, Passage 4*

Neurobiologists once believed that the workings of the brain were guided exclusively by electrical signals; according to this theory, communication between neurons (brain cells) is possible because electrical
(5) impulses travel from one neuron to the next by literally leaping across synapses (gaps between neurons). But many neurobiologists puzzled over how this leaping across synapses might be achieved, and as early as 1904 some speculated that electrical impulses
(10) are transmitted between neurons chemically rather than electrically. According to this alternative theory, the excited neuron secretes a chemical called a neurotransmitter that binds with its corresponding receptor molecule in the receiving neuron. This binding
(15) of the neurotransmitter renders the neuron permeable to ions, and as the ions move into the receiving neuron they generate an electrical impulse that runs through the cell; the electrical impulse is thereby transmitted to the receiving neuron.
(20)    This theory has gradually won acceptance in the scientific community, but for a long time little was known about the mechanism by which neurotransmitters manage to render the receiving neuron permeable to ions. In fact, some scientists
(25) remained skeptical of the theory because they had trouble imagining how the binding of a chemical to a receptor at the cell surface could influence the flow of ions through the cell membrane. Recently, however, researchers have gathered enough evidence for a
(30) convincing explanation: that the structure of receptors plays the pivotal role in mediating the conversion of chemical signals into electrical activity.

The new evidence shows that receptors for neurotransmitters contain both a neurotransmitter
(35) binding site and a separate region that functions as a channel for ions; attachment of the neurotransmitter to the binding site causes the receptor to change shape and so results in the opening of its channel component. Several types of receptors have been isolated that
(40) conform to this structure, among them the receptors for acetylcholine, gamma-aminobutyric acid (GABA), glycine, and serotonin. These receptors display enough similarities to constitute a family, known collectively as neurotransmitter-gated ion channels.
(45)    It has also been discovered that each of the receptors in this family comes in several varieties so that, for example, a GABA receptor in one part of the brain has slightly different properties than a GABA receptor in another part of the brain. This discovery is
(50) medically significant because it raises the possibility of the highly selective treatment of certain brain disorders. As the precise effect on behavior of every variety of each neurotransmitter-gated ion channel is

deciphered, pharmacologists may be able to design
(55) drugs targeted to specific receptors on defined categories of neurons that will selectively impede or enhance these effects. Such drugs could potentially help ameliorate any number of debilitating conditions, including mood disorders, tissue damage associated
(60) with stroke, or Alzheimer's disease.

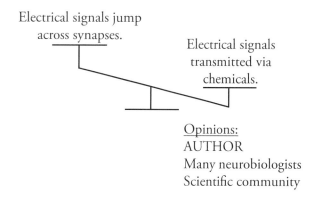

Electrical signals jump across synapses.

Electrical signals transmitted via chemicals.

Opinions:
AUTHOR
Many neurobiologists
Scientific community

Support for:
-New research
-Drug therapy possibilities

*Note that we've placed the author under the right side of the scale. The author's opinion is subtle, but lines 28–32 give us an indication that the author has been "convinced."*

*This passage ends with a "curved tail" (discussed earlier in the book). The central argument is used as a springboard into the implications for drug therapy and treatments for diseases.*

**SYNTHESIS**

21. Which one of the following most completely and accurately states the main point of the passage?

(A) Evidence shows that the workings of the brain are guided, not by electrical signals, but by chemicals, and that subtle differences among the receptors for these chemicals may permit the selective treatment of certain brain disorders.

(B) Evidence shows that the workings of the brain are guided, not by electrical signals, but by chemicals, and that enough similarities exist among these chemicals to allow scientists to classify them as a family.

(C) Evidence shows that electrical impulses are transmitted between neurons chemically rather than electrically, and that enough similarities exist among these chemicals to allow scientists to classify them as a family.

(D) Evidence shows that electrical impulses are transmitted between neurons chemically rather than electrically, and that subtle differences among the receptors for these chemicals may permit the selective treatment of certain brain disorders.

(E) Evidence shows that receptor molecules in the brain differ subtly from one another, and that these differences can be exploited to treat certain brain disorders through the use of drugs that selectively affect particular parts of the brain.

**Referenced text:**
…leaping across synapses might be achieved, and as early as 1904 some speculated that electrical impulses
(10) are transmitted between neurons chemically rather than electrically.

…receptor in another part of the brain. This discovery is
(50) medically significant because it raises the possibility of the highly selective treatment of certain brain disorders.

**Comment:**
*Knowing the argument, and where the author stands, is very important for this question. The first part of answer (D), the correct answer, is basically the right side of our scale! Be careful with (A) and (B): "workings of the brain" is too general. The passage*

*discusses only one specific process within the brain: the transfer of electrical impulses from neuron to neuron. Remember, when more than one answer looks good, be sure to examine the small details of each.*

**IDENTIFICATION**

23. Each of the following statements is affirmed by the passage EXCEPT:

(A) The secretion of certain chemicals plays a role in neuron communication.

(B) The flow of ions through neurons plays a role in neuron communication.

(C) The binding of neurotransmitters to receptors plays a role in neuron communication.

(D) The structure of receptors on neuron surfaces plays a role in neuron communication.

(E) The size of neurotransmitter binding sites on receptors plays a role in neuron communication.

**Referenced text:**
(10) …transmitted between neurons chemically rather than electrically. According to this alternative theory, the excited neuron secretes a chemical called a neurotransmitter that binds with its corresponding receptor molecule in the receiving neuron. This binding
(15) of the neurotransmitter renders the neuron permeable to ions, and as the ions move into the receiving neuron…

(30) …convincing explanation: that the structure of receptors plays the pivotal role in mediating the conversion of chemical signals into electrical activity.

**Comment:**
*Identification questions asked in the "EXCEPT" format tend to require the most time and energy. If you don't have a strong initial impression, you must arrive at the correct answer by finding the other four in the text.*

MANHATTAN
LSAT

## INFERENCE

24. The author most likely uses the phrase "defined categories of neurons" in lines 55–56 in order to refer to neurons that

(A) possess channels for ions
(B) respond to drug treatment
(C) contain receptor molecules
(D) influence particular brain functions
(E) react to binding by neurotransmitters

### Referenced text:

(50) ...receptor in another part of the brain. This discovery is medically significant because it raises the possibility of the highly selective treatment of certain brain disorders. As the precise effect on behavior of every variety of each neurotransmitter-gated ion channel is

(55) deciphered, pharmacologists may be able to design drugs targeted to specific receptors on defined categories of neurons that will selectively impede or enhance these effects. Such drugs could potentially

(60) help ameliorate any number of debilitating conditions, including mood disorders, tissue damage associated with stroke, or Alzheimer's disease.

### Comment:

*While the author doesn't explicitly state what she means by "defined categories of neurons," we can infer the meaning from the surrounding text. An understanding of context is crucial here. The term "defined categories of neurons" is mentioned in the context of treating different types of brain disorders.*

## SYNTHESIS

25. Which one of the following most accurately describes the organization of the passage?

(A) explanation of a theory; presentation of evidence in support of the theory; presentation of evidence in opposition to the theory; argument in favor of rejecting the theory; discussion of the implication of rejecting the theory

(B) explanation of a theory; presentation of evidence in support of the theory; explanation of an alternative theory; presentation of information to support the alternative theory; discussion of an experiment that can help determine which theory is correct

(C) explanation of a theory; description of an obstacle to the theory's general acceptance; presentation of an explanation that helps the theory overcome the obstacle; discussion of a further implication of the theory

(D) explanation of a theory; description of an obstacle to the theory's general acceptance; argument that the obstacle is insurmountable and that the theory should be rejected; discussion of the implications of rejecting the theory

(E) explanation of a theory; description of how the theory came to win scientific acceptance; presentation of new information that challenges the theory; modification of the theory to accommodate the new information; discussion of an implication of the modification.

### Comment:

*This is another Synthesis question for which a strong structural understanding of the passage relative to the argument is of great benefit. The other choices may describe one or two parts of the passage accurately, but (C) is the only choice that describes all parts of the passage correctly.*

5

**_October 2003, Section 4, Passage 2_**

Countee Cullen (Countee Leroy Porter, 1903–1946) was one of the foremost poets of the Harlem Renaissance, the movement of African American writers, musicians, and artists centered in the
(5) Harlem section of New York City during the 1920's. Beginning with his university years, Cullen strove to establish himself as an author of romantic poetry on abstract, universal topics such as love and death. Believing poetry should consist of "lofty thoughts
(10) beautifully expressed," Cullen preferred controlled poetic forms. He used European forms such as sonnets and devices such as quatrains, couplets, and conventional rhyme, and he frequently employed classical allusions and Christian religious imagery,
(15) which were most likely the product both of his university education and of his upbringing as the adopted son of a Methodist Episcopal reverend.

Some literary critics have praised Cullen's skill at writing European-style verse, finding, for example, in
(20) "The Ballad of the Brown Girl" an artful use of diction and a rhythm and sonority that allow him to capture the atmosphere typical of the English ballad form of past centuries. Others have found Cullen's use of European verse forms and techniques unsuited to treating
(25) political or racial themes, such as the themes in "Uncle Jim," in which a young man is told by his uncle of the different experiences of African Americans and whites in United States society, or "Incident," which relates the experience of an eight-year-old child who hears a racial
(30) slur. One such critic complained that Cullen's persona as expressed in his work sometimes seems to vacillate between aesthete and spokesperson for racial issues. But Cullen himself rejected this dichotomy, maintaining that his interest in romantic
(35) poetry was quite compatible with his concern over racial issues. He drew a distinction between poetry of solely political intent and his own work, which he believed reflected his identify as an African American. As the heartfelt expression of his personality
(40) accomplished by means of careful attention to his chosen craft, his work could not help but do so.

Explicit references to racial matters do in fact decline in Cullen's later work, but not because he felt any less passionately about these matters. Rather,
(45) Cullen increasingly focused on the religious dimension of his poetry. In "The Black Christ," in which the poet imagines the death and resurrection of a rural African American, and "Heritage," which expresses the tension between the poet's identification with Christian
(50) traditions and his desire to stay close to his African heritage, Cullen's thoughts on race were subsumed

within what he conceived of as broader and more urgent questions about the suffering and redemption of the soul. Nonetheless, Cullen never abandoned his commitment to the importance of racial issues, reflecting on one occasion that he felt "actuated by a
(55) strong sense of race consciousness" that "grows upon me, I find, as I grow older."

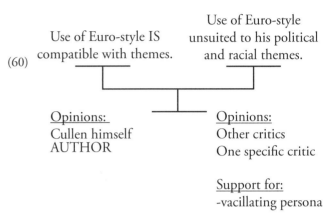

(60)

*Note the very subtle indication of the author's opinion in lines 40–43. Also note the "curved tail" in the last paragraph. In the last paragraph, the author moves beyond the central argument to discuss trends in Cullen's later work.*

**SYNTHESIS**

7. Which one of the following most accurately states the main point of the passage?

(A) While much of Cullen's poetry deals with racial issues, in his later work he became less concerned with racial matters and increasingly interested in writing poetry with a religious dimension.

(B) While Cullen used European verse forms and his later poems increasingly addressed religious themes, his poetry never abandoned a concern for racial issues.

(C) Though Cullen used European verse forms, he acknowledged that these forms were not very well suited to treating political or racial themes.

(D) Despite the success of Cullen's poetry at dealing with racial issues, Cullen's primary goal was to re-create the atmosphere that characterized the English ballad.

(E) The religious dimension throughout Cullen's poetry complemented his focus on racial issues by providing the context within which these issues could be understood.

**Referenced text:**

…Believing poetry should consist of "lofty thoughts
(10) beautifully expressed," Cullen preferred controlled poetic forms. He used European forms such as sonnets and devices such as quatrains, couplets, and conventional rhyme…

…decline in Cullen's later work, but not because he felt any less passionately about these matters. Rather,
(45) Cullen increasingly focused on the religious dimension of his poetry.

…the soul. Nonetheless, Cullen never abandoned his
(55) commitment to the importance of racial issues…

**Comment:**

*This is another Synthesis question for which the correct answer is not ideal, but is the best available. (B) correctly brings together elements mentioned in different parts of the passage. (A) incorrectly states that Cullen became less concerned with racial issues in his later work. (C) is in direct contradiction to Cullen's actual opinion (we can see this in our scale). Neither (D) nor (E) is supported by information in the passage.*

**INFERENCE**

8. Given the information in the passage, which one of the following most closely exemplifies Cullen's conception of poetry?

(A) a sonnet written with careful attention to the conventions of the form to re-create the atmosphere of sixteenth-century English poetry

(B) a sonnet written with deliberate disregard for the conventions of the form to illustrate the perils of political change

(C) a sonnet written to explore the aesthetic impact of radical innovations in diction, rhythm, and sonority

(D) a sonnet written with great stylistic freedom to express the emotional upheaval associated with romantic love

(E) a sonnet written with careful attention to the conventions of the form expressing feelings about the inevitability of death

**Referenced text:**

…Beginning with his university years, Cullen strove to establish himself as an author of romantic poetry on abstract, universal topics such as love and death. Believing poetry should consist of "lofty thoughts
(10) beautifully expressed," Cullen preferred controlled poetic forms. He used European forms such as sonnets and devices such as quatrains, couplets, and conventional rhyme…

**Comment:**

*(E) is fairly provable based on the text. Remember, correct answers to Inference questions won't be explicitly stated in the text, but they can generally be inferred, without making any additional assumptions or logical leaps, from specific lines in the text.*

5

## IDENTIFICATION

9. Which one of the following is NOT identified by the author of the passage as characteristic of Cullen's poetry?

(A) It often deals with abstract, universal subject matter.
(B) It often employs rhyme, classical allusions, and religious imagery.
(C) It avoids traditional poetic forms in favor of formal experimentation.
(D) It sometimes deals explicitly with racial issues.
(E) It eventually subsumed racial issues into a discussion of religious issues.

**Referenced text:**
(5) ...Harlem section of New York City during the 1920's. Beginning with his university years, Cullen strove to establish himself as an author of romantic poetry on abstract, universal topics.

(12) ...couplets, and conventional rhyme, and he frequently employed classical allusions and Christian religious imagery...

(30) ...themes in "Uncle Jim," in which a young man is told by his uncle of the different experiences of African Americans and whites in United States society, or "Incident," which relates the experience of an eight-year-old child who hears a
(35) racial slur.

...any less passionately about these matters. Rather,
(45) Cullen increasingly focused on the religious dimension of his poetry.

**Comment:**
*This is very similar to an "EXCEPT" question. (C) jumps out as being incongruous relative to the rest of the passage (Cullen borrowed from European tradition, and there is no mention of his experimenting). Because of this, we can scan the text to make sure it is not there. However, if we were uncertain about (C), we could also get to the right answer by finding the other four in the text, as we've done above.*

## IDENTIFICATION

10. The passage suggests which one of the following about Cullen's use of controlled poetic forms?

(A) Cullen used controlled poetic forms because he believed they provided the best means to beautiful poetic expression.
(B) Cullen's interest in religious themes naturally led him to use controlled poetic forms.
(C) Only the most controlled poetic forms allowed Cullen to address racial issues in his poems.
(D) Cullen had rejected the less controlled poetic forms he was exposed to prior to his university years.
(E) Less controlled poetic forms are better suited to poetry that addresses racial or political issues.

**Referenced text:**
...Believing poetry should consist of "lofty thoughts
(10) beautifully expressed," Cullen preferred controlled poetic forms...

**Comment:**
*It's easy to overthink a question like this. Don't waste time comparing the meaning of certain answer choices to that of others. Instead, spend that time looking for proof in the text that will validate a particular answer choice.*

**_October 2003, Section 4, Passage 4_**

Although philanthropy—the volunteering of private resources for humanitarian purposes—reached its apex in England in the late nineteenth century, modern commentators have articulated two major
(5) criticisms of the philanthropy that was a mainstay of England's middle-class Victorian society. The earlier criticism is that such philanthropy was even by the later nineteenth century obsolete, since industrialism had already created social problems that were beyond the
(10) scope of small, private voluntary efforts. Indeed, these problems required substantial legislative action by the state. Unemployment, for example, was not the result of a failure of diligence on the part of workers or a failure of compassion on the part of employers, nor
(15) could it be solved by well-wishing philanthropists.

The more recent charge holds that Victorian philanthropy was by its very nature a self-serving exercise carried out by philanthropists at the expense of those whom they were ostensibly serving. In this view,
(20) philanthropy was a means of flaunting one's power and position in a society that placed great emphasis on status, or even a means of cultivating social connections that could lead to economic rewards. Further, if philanthropy is seen as serving the interests
(25) of individual philanthropists, so it may be seen as serving the interests of their class. According to this "social control" thesis, philanthropists, in professing to help the poor, were encouraging in them such values as prudence, thrift, and temperance, values perhaps
(30) worthy in themselves but also designed to create more productive members of the labor force. Philanthropy, in short, was a means of controlling the labor force and ensuring the continued dominance of the management class.
(35) Modern critics of Victorian philanthropy often use the words "amateurish" or "inadequate" to describe Victorian philanthropy, as though Victorian charity can only be understood as an antecedent to the era of state-sponsored, professionally administered charity. This
(40) assumption is typical of the "Whig fallacy": the tendency to read the past as an inferior prelude to an enlightened present. If most Victorians resisted state control and expended their resources on private, voluntary philanthropies, it could only be, the argument
(45) goes, because of their commitment to a vested interest, or because the administrative apparatus of the state was incapable of coping with the economic and social needs of the time.

This version of history patronizes the Victorians,
(50) who were in fact well aware of their vulnerability to charges of condescension and complacency, but were equally well aware of the potential dangers of state-managed charity. They were perhaps condescending to the poor, but—to use an un-Victorian metaphor—they
(55) put their money where their mouths were, and gave of their careers and lives as well.

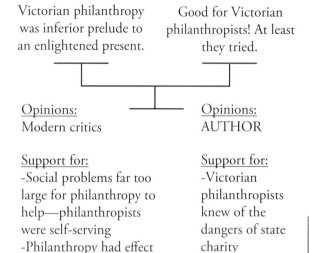

Victorian philanthropy was inferior prelude to an enlightened present.

Good for Victorian philanthropists! At least they tried.

Opinions: Modern critics

Opinions: AUTHOR

Support for:
-Social problems far too large for philanthropy to help—philanthropists were self-serving
-Philanthropy had effect of controlling labor class

Support for:
-Victorian philanthropists knew of the dangers of state charity
-They sacrificed

*The central argument in this passage doesn't reveal itself until the last paragraph! All the more reason to remain flexible, to constantly scrutinize your understanding, to guess and reasess as you read.*

**5**

**5**

## SYNTHESIS

21. Which one of the following best summarizes the main idea of the passage?

(A) While the motives of individual practitioners have been questioned by modern commentators, Victorian philanthropy successfully dealt with the social ills of nineteenth-century England.

(B) Philanthropy, inadequate to deal with the massive social and economic problems of the twentieth century, has slowly been replaced by state-sponsored charity.

(C) The practice of reading the past as a prelude to an enlightened present has fostered revisionist views of many institutions, among them Victorian philanthropy.

(D) Although modern commentators have perceived Victorian philanthropy as either inadequate or self-serving, the theoretical bias behind these criticisms leads to an incorrect interpretation of history.

(E) Victorian philanthropists, aware of public resentment of their self-congratulatory attitude, used devious methods to camouflage their self serving motives.

**Referenced text:**

(6) …England's middle-class Victorian society. The earlier criticism is that such philanthropy was even by the later nineteenth century obsolete…

(16) The more recent charge holds that Victorian philanthropy was by its very nature a self-serving…

(35) Modern critics of Victorian philanthropy often use the words "amateurish" or "inadequate" to describe Victorian philanthropy, as though Victorian charity can only be understood as an antecedent to the era of state-sponsored, professionally administered charity…

(50) This version of history patronizes the Victorians, who were in fact well aware of their vulnerability to charges of condescension and complacency, but were equally well aware of the potential dangers of state managed charity.

**Comment:**

*(D) correctly combines different elements of the passage into a cohesive whole that matches the argument scale and represents the author's opinion.*

## INFERENCE

22. According to the passage, which one of the following is true of both modern criticisms made about Victorian philanthropy?

(A) Both criticisms attribute dishonorable motives to those privileged individuals who engaged in private philanthropy.

(B) Both criticisms presuppose that the social rewards of charitable activity outweighed the economic benefits.

(C) Both criticisms underemphasize the complacency and condescension demonstrated by the Victorians.

(D) Both criticisms suggest that government involvement was necessary to cure social ills.

(E) Both criticisms take for granted the futility of efforts by private individuals to enhance their social status by means of philanthropy.

**Referenced text:**

(5) …modern commentators have articulated two major criticisms of the philanthropy that was a mainstay of England's middle-class Victorian society.

(35) Modern critics of Victorian philanthropy often use the words "amateurish" or "inadequate" to describe Victorian philanthropy, as though Victorian charity can only be understood as an antecedent to the era of state-sponsored, professionally administered charity…

**Comment:**

*This is a challenging question, and the correct answer is one that is difficult to anticipate. Still, we can see that it is fairly provable based on the text. If Victorian philanthropy is viewed as an inadequate precursor to state-sponsored charity, we can infer that the critics feel state sponsorship is required of wiser charitable actions. Some of the other answers are attractive because they are mentioned in relation to one criticism or the other, but only (D) refers to both.*

## INFERENCE

25. It can be inferred from the passage that a social control theorist would be most likely to agree with which one of the following statements concerning the motives of Victorian philanthropists?

(A)  Victorian philanthropists were driven more by the desire for high social status than by the hope of economic gain.

(B)  Victorian philanthropists encouraged such values as thrift and temperance in order to instill in the working class the same acquisitiveness that characterized the management class.

(C)  Though basically well-intentioned, Victorian philanthropists faced problems that were far beyond the scope of private charitable organizations.

(D)  By raising the living standards of the poor, Victorian philanthropists also sought to improve the intellectual status of the poor.

(E)  Victorian philanthropists see philanthropy as a means to an end rather than as an end in itself.

**Referenced text:**
…According to this
"social control" thesis, philanthropists, in professing to help the poor, were encouraging in them such values as prudence, thrift, and temperance, values perhaps
(30) worthy in themselves but also designed to create more productive members of the labor force. Philanthropy, in short, was a means of controlling the labor force and ensuring the continued dominance of the management class.

**Comment:**
*Several of the wrong answers to this question make logical sense, but are not provable by the text itself. The text tells us that these philanthropists were looking forward to secondary, self-preserving ramifications of their seemingly selfless acts.*

## SYNTHESIS

26. Which of the following best describes the organization of the passage?

(A)  Two related positions are discussed, then both are subjected to the same criticism.

(B)  Two opposing theories are outlined, then a synthesis between the two is proposed.

(C)  A position is stated, and two differing evaluations of it are given.

(D)  Three examples of the same logical inconsistency are given.

(E)  A theory is outlined, and two supporting examples are given.

**Referenced text:**
…its apex in England in the late nineteenth century, modern commentators have articulated two major
(5) criticisms of the philanthropy that was a mainstay of England's middle-class Victorian society. The earlier criticism is that such philanthropy was even by the later nineteenth century obsolete, …

(16)     The more recent charge holds that Victorian philanthropy was by its very nature a self-serving…

(35)     Modern critics of Victorian philanthropy often use the words "amateurish" or "inadequate" to describe Victorian philanthropy, as though Victorian charity can only be understood as an antecedent to the era of state-sponsored, professionally administered charity…

     This version of history patronizes the Victorians,
(50) who were in fact well aware of their vulnerability to charges of condescension and complacency, but were equally well aware of the potential dangers of state managed charity.

**Comment:**
*Some of the answers are obviously wrong, and some mention only limited parts of the passage. (A), though not very insightful, does correctly represent disparate parts of the passage. (A) is basically a rewording of our scale!*

# Conclusion

## Interpreting Your Results

The previous passages collectively contained four Identification questions, six Inference questions, and six Synthesis questions. Take a moment and give yourself a score on all three question types.

| IDENTIFICATION | INFERENCE | SYNTHESIS |
|:---:|:---:|:---:|
| 4 /4 | 0 /6 | 3 /6 |

Though this is a relatively small sample, marked differences in performance on different question types should give you some indication as to which parts of your process are working well, and which parts are not. Think about why you are missing certain question types, and adjust accordingly. For example, a weakness on Synthesis questions may point to a rushed initial read, one in which you didn't consider overall argument structure. A weakness on Identification questions may be a result of your answering process—perhaps you are relying on gut instinct instead of taking the time to go back into the text to find your proof. A weakness on Inference questions may also stem from a failure to find supporting text in the passage. In addition, you may be making invalid assumptions or extrapolations. Don't infer too much!

Looking at the results in couples may also be of interest. If you are strong at both identification and inference, but not synthesis, perhaps that is evidence that you are not reading towards a generalized understanding, and that you are getting lost in the details in your initial read. If you are strong at identification and synthesis but not inference, perhaps you need to reset your gauge in terms of understanding the type of deduction processes the LSAT expects of you. If you are strong at synthesis but weak at identification and inference, you may need to do a better job of finding corroborating evidence.

As we go forward, continue to use your results to fine-tune your process on practice exams, and you should continue to see improvements in your score.

MANHATTAN
LSAT

# Chapter 6
## *of*
## Reading Comprehension

# Incorrect Answers

# The Search for Incorrect Answers

Now that you know what you are looking for in a correct answer, how do you find it, exactly? Question prompts generally set up scenarios for which any number of different answers might be correct. Therefore:

**For the vast majority of LSAT Reading Comprehension problems, you should arrive at the correct answer by eliminating incorrect answers.**

One of the defining characteristics of a 170+ test-taker is the ability to eliminate answer choices confidently and accurately. Let's look at some common characteristics of two different test-takers:

| 170+ | Average Test-Taker |
|---|---|
| Starts by actively seeking to eliminate wrong answers. | Starts by looking for the right answer. |
| Uses an understanding of incorrect answer characteristics to confidently eliminate obviously incorrect answers. | Uses instinct, or "gut sense," to evaluate answers. |
| Spends the majority of his or her time breaking down and double-checking the most attractive answer choices. | Wastes time overthinking obviously incorrect choices, and doesn't have time to carefully examine the most likely possibilities. |
| Rarely returns to an answer that he or she eliminates. | Eliminates some answers with certainty and some without, and often has to go back and reexamine every answer choice again. |

It's okay if you feel like you fall into the "average test-taker" category right now. The key is to actively work towards making the exam more familiar, and to actively work towards attaining the characteristics of the 170+ test-taker.

For most, the conversion is a gradual process. Developing good test-taking skills is not unlike developing a good jump shot. In order to develop a good jump shot, you need two things: a consistent, effective form, and practice. Without a consistent form, you will shoot every shot differently, and improvement will be hard to come by. Without practice, your form will never become intuitive, and therefore won't ever be fully effective, especially under pressure.

There are four elements essential to having the right "form" when it comes to answering LSAT Reading Comprehension questions:

1. An active and accurate first read that focuses on the structure of the passage relative to a central argument
2. An elimination process that saves time and helps you narrow down your focus until you arrive at the right answer
3. An understanding of how the LSAT writes incorrect answer choices
4. A solid sense of how correct answers are structured

So far, we've discussed how to read the passage, and what makes an answer choice correct. In this chapter, we will focus on the common characteristics of incorrect choices. As you continue to practice

MANHATTAN
LSAT

passages, focus on your form. When you miss a question, try to be as specific as possible about why. It's not enough to say to yourself, "I misunderstood this," or "I'm bad at synthesis problems." Relate every weakness to your form and your understanding of the test, and actively seek out ways to improve.

# The Characteristics of Incorrect Answers

Imagine that the LSAT test writer starts out every question by first listing five *correct* answer choices. One by one, she introduces elements into four of the answers that will distort these answers in one way or another. The one answer that remains untainted will be the one that is correct.

Most test-takers don't give a lot of thought as to why answers are incorrect. However, if you can recognize the common characteristics of incorrect answers, and if you practice enough to incorporate this recognition into your intuitive process, you will fundamentally change how you read the LSAT. Answers will jump out at you as being incorrect, and you will always be able to zero in on the most challenging or subtle issue in any question.

**Answers on the LSAT are not incorrect in haphazard ways. They are incorrect because of common, concrete flaws.** We categorize these flaws into three categories: Interpretation, Scope, and Degree. Though we will discuss question types in which these flaws occur most often, be aware that they can appear at any point, for any type of question.

## Interpretation

Answers incorrect because of interpretation issues generally translate the information in the text incorrectly in one of two ways:

> **1. Contradiction.** The answer choice states the exact opposite of what is written in the text.
> **2. Unsupported.** The answer choice jumps to an interpretation that requires a logical leap that is unsupported by the text.

Often the answers to **Inference questions** are incorrect because of interpretation issues. We are tempted to pick answers that are the complete opposite of the text if we are uncertain about where opinions fall on the argument scale. We are often tempted by answers that are unsupported by the text because we find these choices, like the text, challenging to understand. If we sense that we are missing something, we might feel that the right answer should make a leap in logic, going beyond what we understand. That is rarely the case. As we saw in the previous chapter, all answers are fairly provable based on the text, and they never require a giant leap in logic.

## Scope

We define scope as the range of subject matter that is discussed. There are two main types of scope issues:

> **1. Out of scope.** The answer choice is outside the scope of the passage (it involves elements that were not mentioned in the passage).
> **2. Narrow Scope.** The scope of the answer doesn't match the scope of the question (the question asks about the passage as a whole, but the answer relates to only one paragraph, for example).

6

Often the answers to **Identification questions** are incorrect because they are outside the scope of the passage, and often the answers to Synthesis questions are incorrect because the scope of the answers doesn't match the scope of the question.

A subcategory of answers with incorrect scope are **half-scope** answers, which pertain specifically to **comparative passages** (which we'll discuss in the next chapter). Often questions for comparative passages ask you about what the two passages have in common, and the wrong answers to these questions tend to touch on one passage or the other, but not both.

## Degree

Degree issues show up in two forms:

> **1. Incorrect degree: opinion.** Think of opinions as sitting on a spectrum: disgust, dislike, objectivity, uncertainty, slight favor, like, and love. An incorrect answer choice of this type will misrepresent the degree of an opinion stated in the passage.
> **2. Incorrect degree: modifier.** Think of a spectrum of modifiers that define number: one, a few, some, many, most, all. LSAT answer choices are often incorrect because a modifier misrepresents the degree of a certain number.

Let's use a simple truncated example to illustrate each type of common flaw.

## Incorrect Answer Examples

Take a moment to read the following truncated passage. Then consider the abbreviated questions and answers that follow.

> Jazz music is rooted in a history similar to that of America itself: a history of confluence. The jazz first played in New Orleans in the early 1900s borrowed heavily from European and West African musical traditions.
>
> Musicologists who argue that jazz is a purely American art form often point to its genesis in New Orleans as evidence for this counter-perspective. The irony, however, is that the essence of America lies in the plurality of its roots. To deny the rich and complex history of jazz, and the true origins of the art form, is in effect denying the very aspects of the art form that make it undeniably American.

## 1. INTERPRETATION Issues

*Contradiction (opposite of what was stated in text)*

The author of the passage would be most likely to agree with which one of the following statements?

(X̸) The jazz music first played in New Orleans was a purely American art form.

*Unsupported (infers too far beyond text)*

The author of the passage would be most likely to agree with which one of the following statements?

(B̸) Jazz music was influenced more by European traditions than by West African traditions.

Notice that the answer choice is not only wrong, it is the complete **opposite** of what is in the passage ("The jazz first played in New Orleans in the early 1900s borrowed heavily from European and West African musical traditions."). This is a surprisingly common characteristic in incorrect choices; the best way to avoid getting fooled by these answers is to understand the central argument, and to assign opinions, especially the author's opinion, to the correct side of the argument.

This answer may initially be appealing because it contains terms that are in the text (European and West African traditions); however, the answer takes an **unwarranted leap in logic.** The original text mentions both European and West African traditions as elements that influenced American Jazz, but gives no indication whatsoever as to which one was more of an influence relative to the other. Test-takers often fall for these answers on passages they had a difficult time understanding as a whole. Don't be tempted to pick answers that stretch the text just because the text was confusing.

## 2. SCOPE Issues

*Out of scope (beyond what is discussed in the text)*

Which of the following most accurately states the main point of the passage?

(X̸) Like rock music, jazz music borrowed from many pre-existing musical traditions.

Rock music isn't mentioned in the text. Therefore, the main point of the passage cannot involve a comparison between rock music and jazz.

*Narrow scope (scope of answer doesn't match scope of question)*

Which of the following most accurately states the main point of the passage?

(B̸) The essence of America lies in the richness and diversity of its roots.

This statement is indeed true according to the passage, but it is just one part of a larger argument. The main thrust of the passage is about whether or not jazz music is a purely American art form. In this case, the scope of the answer doesn't match the scope of the question.

It's possible that scope may work in reverse as well. That is, an answer will apply more generally to the text as a whole, and be incorrect because the question will apply more specifically to one section.

6

MANHATTAN
LSAT

However, these situations are less common.

### 3. DEGREE Issues

*Incorrect degree: opinion (the scale of an opinion is incorrectly represented)*

Which of the following most accurately describes the author's attitude toward the musicologists mentioned in the passage?

(X) complete disgust

Though the author disagrees with these musicologists, the text certainly does not indicate as strong an emotion as "complete disgust." A nuanced, and complete understanding of the author's opinion is the key to recognizing these errors.

*Incorrect degree: modifier (the scale of the subject matter has been incorrectly represented)*

Which of the following is most directly supported by the passage?

(X) All musicologists believe that jazz music is a purely American art form.

The primary problem here is the word "all." Musicologists have been mentioned, but the text doesn't give any hint that all musicologists share a common opinion. Be on the lookout for incorrect representations of these types of modifiers. The more absolute and extreme they are (all, never, every, each, none, etc.), the more suspicious you should be. This is a very common error in incorrect answer choices.

## Practical Applications of Knowing the Characteristics of Incorrect Answer Choices

We want to make it clear now: you should not consciously categorize every incorrect answer on the real exam. That would be a waste of your very limited time. However, a thorough understanding of how the LSAT makes an answer incorrect should help you in two ways:

**1. You will get more out of your review.** Go back to problems you missed and see if you can categorize the wrong answers you picked. Most people will see some commonality in the incorrect answers they select (often fail to notice differences in degree, for example). If you notice these issues, it's much easier to address them.

**2. You will hone your intuition.** Let's see how an understanding of incorrect answer characteristics can help refine your intuition:

| *What makes answers incorrect* | *What instincts this should inspire* |
| --- | --- |
| **Interpretation:** contradiction | Need to have a clear understanding of what role opinions and evidence play relative to the central argument. |
| **Interpretation:** unsupported | Need to avoid picking answers that "sound good." I should verify all answers I am not 100% sure of by rereading the text. |
| **Scope:** out of scope | I shouldn't try to infer too much, or take big "logic leaps," even when I don't completely understand the text. |
| **Scope:** narrow scope | For general questions, I need an answer that relates different parts of the passage together. |
| **Degree:** opinion | I should continuously try to gauge the levels of the opinions mentioned in the passage. |
| **Degree:** modifiers | I should pay attention to small words (some vs. most, etc.) that define a group. |

At first, you'll concentrate on developing these instincts. Then, you'll begin to notice that incorrect answers jump out a bit more quickly for you. After a while, you'll spot the obviously wrong answers almost instantly as you read them. You want to do the hard work of analyzing and categorizing wrong answers now so that when you take the exam the process of eliminating bad choices will be almost automatic.

**6**

# DRILL IT: Incorrect Answer Characteristics

Read the following passage and answer the questions to the best of your ability. Do this *untimed*. For every wrong answer, take the time to decide *why* it is wrong: interpretation (I), scope (S), or degree (D). Some answers are wrong for multiple reasons.

### October 2003, Section 4, Passage 1

In a recent court case, a copy-shop owner was accused of violating copyright law when, in the preparation of "course packs"—materials photocopied from books and journals and packaged as readings for
(5) particular university courses—he copied materials without obtaining permission from or paying sufficient fees to the publishers. As the owner of five small copy shops serving several educational institutions in the area, he argued, as have others in the photocopy
(10) business, that the current process for obtaining permissions is time-consuming, cumbersome, and expensive. He also maintained that course packs, which are ubiquitous in higher education, allow professors to assign important readings in books and journals too
(15) costly for students to be expected to purchase individually. While the use of copyrighted material for teaching purposes is typically protected by certain provisions of copyright law, this case was unique in that the copying of course packs was done by a copy
(20) shop and at a profit.

Copyright law outlines several factors involved in determining whether the use of copyrighted material is protected, including: whether it is for commercial or nonprofit purposes; the nature of the copyrighted work;
(25) the length and importance of the excerpt used in relation to the entire work; and the effect of its use on the work's potential market value. In bringing suit, the publishers held that other copy-shop owners would cease paying permission fees, causing the potential
(30) value of the copyrighted works of scholarship to diminish. Nonetheless, the court decided that this reasoning did not demonstrate that course packs would have a sufficiently adverse effect on the current or potential market of the copyrighted works or on the
(35) value of the copyrighted works themselves. The court instead ruled that since the copies were for educational purposes, the fact that the copy-shop owner had profited from making the course packs did not prevent him from receiving protection under the law.
(40) According to the court, the owner had not exploited copyrighted material because his fee was not based on the content of the works he copied; he charged by the page, regardless of whether the content was copyrighted.
(45)     In the court's view, the business of producing and selling course packs is more properly seen as the

exploitation of professional copying technologies and a result of the inability of academic parties to reproduce printed materials efficiently, not the exploitation of
(50) these copyrighted materials themselves. The court held that copyright laws do not prohibit professors and students, who may make copies for themselves, from using the photoreproduction services of a third party in order to obtain those same copies at a lesser cost.

1. Which one of the following most accurately states the main point of the passage?

(A) A court recently ruled that a copy shop that makes course packs does not illegally exploit copyrighted materials but rather it legally exploits the efficiency of professional photocopying technology.

(B) A court recently ruled that course packs are protected by copyright law because their price is based solely on the number of pages in each pack.

(C) A court recently ruled that the determining factors governing the copyrights of material used in course packs are how the material is to be used, the nature of the material itself, and the length of the copied excerpts.

(D) A recent court ruling limits the rights of publishers to seek suit against copy shops that make course packs from copyrighted material.

(E) Exceptions to copyright law are made when copyrighted material is used for educational purposes and no party makes a substantial profit from the material.

2. In lines 23–27, the author lists several of the factors used to determine whether copyrighted material is protected by law primarily to

(A) demonstrate why the copy-shop owner was exempt from copyright law in this case

(B) explain the charges the publishers brought against the copy-shop owner

(C) illustrate a major flaw in the publishers' reasoning

(D) defend the right to use copyrighted materials for educational purposes

(E) provide the legal context for the arguments presented in the case

3. The copy-shop owner as described in the passage would be most likely to agree with which one of the following statements?

(A) The potential market value of a copyrighted work should be calculated to include the impact on sales due to the use of the work in course packs.

(B) Publishers are always opposed to the preparation and sale of course packs.

(C) More copy shops would likely seek permissions from publishers if the process for obtaining permissions were not so cumbersome and expensive.

(D) Certain provisions of copyright law need to be rewritten to apply to all possible situations.

(E) Copy shops make more of a profit from the preparation and sale of course packs than from other materials.

4. The information in the passage provides the most support for which one of the following statements about copyright law?

(A) Copyright law can be one of the most complex areas of any legal system.

(B) Courts have been inconsistent in their interpretations of certain provisions of copyright law.

(C) The number of the kinds of materials granted protection under copyright law is steadily decreasing.

(D) New practices can compel the courts to refine how copyright law is applied.

(E) Copyright law is primarily concerned with making published materials available for educational use.

5. Which one of the following describes a role most similar to that of professors in the passage who use copy shops to produce course packs?

(A) An artisan generates a legible copy of an old headstone engraving by using charcoal on newsprint and frames and sells high-quality photocopies of it at a crafts market.

(B) A choir director tapes a selection of another well-known choir's best pieces and sends it to a recording studio to be reproduced in a sellable package for use by members of her choir.

(C) A grocer makes several kinds of sandwiches that sell for less than similar sandwiches from a nearby upscale cafe.

(D) A professional graphic artist prints reproductions of several well-known paintings at an exhibit to sell at the museum's gift shop.

(E) A souvenir store in the center of a city sells miniature bronze renditions of a famous bronze sculpture that the city is noted for displaying.

6. Which one of the following, if true, would have most strengthened the publishers' position in this case?

(A) Course packs for courses that usually have large enrollments had produced a larger profit for the copy-shop owner.

(B) The copy-shop owner had actively solicited professors' orders for course packs.

(C) The revenue generated by the copy shop's sale of course packs had risen significantly within the past few years.

(D) Many area bookstores had reported a marked decrease in the sales of books used for producing course packs.

(E) The publishers had enlisted the support of the authors to verify their claims that the copy-shop owner had not obtained permission.

6

# SOLUTIONS: Incorrect Answer Characteristics

### *October 2003, Section 4, Passage 1*

In a recent court case, a copy-shop owner was accused of violating copyright law when, in the preparation of "course packs"—materials photocopied from books and journals and packaged as readings for
(5) particular university courses—he copied materials without obtaining permission from or paying sufficient fees to the publishers. As the owner of five small copy shops serving several educational institutions in the area, he argued, as have others in the photocopy
(10) business, that the current process for obtaining permissions is time-consuming, cumbersome, and expensive. He also maintained that course packs, which are ubiquitous in higher education, allow professors to assign important readings in books and journals too
(15) costly for students to be expected to purchase individually. While the use of copyrighted material for teaching purposes is typically protected by certain provisions of copyright law, this case was unique in that the copying of course packs was done by a copy
(20) shop and at a profit.

Copyright law outlines several factors involved in determining whether the use of copyrighted material is protected, including: whether it is for commercial or nonprofit purposes; the nature of the copyrighted work;
(25) the length and importance of the excerpt used in relation to the entire work; and the effect of its use on the work's potential market value. In bringing suit, the publishers held that other copy-shop owners would cease paying permission fees, causing the potential
(30) value of the copyrighted works of scholarship to diminish. Nonetheless, the court decided that this reasoning did not demonstrate that course packs would have a sufficiently adverse effect on the current or potential market of the copyrighted works or on the
(35) value of the copyrighted works themselves. The court instead ruled that since the copies were for educational purposes, the fact that the copy-shop owner had profited from making the course packs did not prevent him from receiving protection under the law.
(40) According to the court, the owner had not exploited copyrighted material because his fee was not based on the content of the works he copied; he charged by the page, regardless of whether the content was copyrighted.
(45)     In the court's view, the business of producing and selling course packs is more properly seen as the

exploitation of professional copying technologies and a result of the inability of academic parties to reproduce printed materials efficiently, not the exploitation of
(50) these copyrighted materials themselves. The court held that copyright laws do not prohibit professors and students, who may make copies for themselves, from using the photoreproduction services of a third party in order to obtain those same copies at a lesser cost.

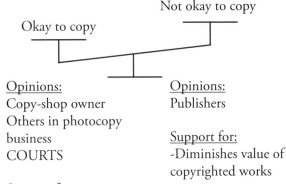

Opinions:
Copy-shop owner
Others in photocopy
business
COURTS

Support for:
-Bad process for
obtaining permissions
-Cheaper for students
-For educational
purposes
-Fee based on copies,
not content
-Exploiting technology,
NOT copyright content

Opinions:
Publishers

Support for:
-Diminishes value of
copyrighted works

*This might be the most straightforward argument we've seen so far! Because it is presented in the context of a court case, the central argument is easy to spot, and the opinions easy to assign.*

*Note that the author remains objective throughout.*

MANHATTAN
LSAT

1. Which one of the following most accurately states the main point of the passage?

(A)  A court recently ruled that a copy shop that makes course packs does not illegally exploit copyrighted materials but rather it legally exploits the efficiency of professional photocopying technology.

 *This is the correct answer.*

(B)  A court recently ruled that course packs are protected by copyright law because their price is based solely on the number of pages in each pack.

 **SCOPE (narrow scope).** *Price based on pages is mentioned, but it certainly does not capture the <u>main</u> point of the passage.*

(C)  A court recently ruled that the determining factors governing the copyrights of material used in course packs are how the material is to be used, the nature of the material itself, and the length of the copied excerpts.

 **SCOPE (narrow scope).** *These factors are mentioned in the passage, but do not capture the main point.*

 **INTERPRETATION (unsupported).** *These elements are mentioned as factors that generally govern copyright law, but the passage does not state that these are the factors that govern the specific issues involving materials in course packs.*

(D)  A recent court ruling limits the rights of publishers to seek suit against copy shops that make course packs from copyrighted material.

 **SCOPE (narrow).** *Again, the ruling is mentioned in the passage, and it will hurt the chances that a publisher will successfully win a case against copy shops (though it's arguable whether you can say it will limit the rights of the publishers), but it is not the main point of the passage.*

(E)  Exceptions to copyright law are made when copyrighted material is used for educational purposes and no party makes a substantial profit from the material.

 **INTERPRETATION (unsupported).** *Educational considerations are not "exceptions" to copyright law; they are a part of copyright law (lines 16–18).*

2. In lines 23–27, the author lists several of the factors used to determine whether copyrighted material is protected by law primarily to

(A)  demonstrate why the copy-shop owner was exempt from copyright law in this case

 **INTERPRETATION (unsupported).** *The list serves as background information to provide context for the argument at hand. The reasons why copy-shop owners are protected come later in the paragraph.*

(B)  explain the charges the publishers brought against the copy-shop owner

 **INTERPRETATION (unsupported).** *The list describes elements involved generally in determining the application of copyright law, but it does not "explain" the charges of the publishers specifically.*

(C)  illustrate a major flaw in the publishers' reasoning

 **DEGREE (opinion).** *Though the publishers lost the case, the author never states that they had "major flaws" in their reasoning. In fact, remember that the author has not even stated his or her opinion!*

 **INTERPRETATION (unsupported).** *Again, this is not the role these lines play in the argument.*

(D)  defend the right to use copyrighted materials for educational purposes

 **INTERPRETATION.** *Again, this is not the role these lines play in the argument.*

(E)  provide the legal context for the arguments presented in the case

 *This is the correct answer. These lines serve as background information for the central argument at hand.*

6

3. The copy-shop owner as described in the passage would be most likely to agree with which one of the following statements?

(A) The potential market value of a copyrighted work should be calculated to include the impact on sales due to the use of the work in course packs.

*INTERPRETATION (unsupported). All of the owner's opinions are clearly stated in the first paragraph. While market value of copyrighted works is discussed in the passage, we don't get any sense for how the owner would recommend calculating market value. Be careful! Elements of this answer might seem familiar and relevant, but you must be sure you're interpreting the information correctly.*

(B) Publishers are always opposed to the preparation and sale of course packs.

*INTERPRETATION (unsupported). Again, while we did read about publishers and course packs, there is nothing in the passage that would support this interpretation.*

*DEGREE (modifier). Furthermore, it is highly unlikely that all publishers will always feel the same way about something.*

(C) More copy shops would likely seek permissions from publishers if the process for obtaining permissions were not so cumbersome and expensive.

*This is the correct answer, and can be directly inferred from the text (lines 10–12).*

(D) Certain provisions of copyright law need to be rewritten to apply to all possible situations.

*SCOPE (out of scope). This is far removed from the opinions of the copy-shop owner that have been mentioned.*

*DEGREE (modifier). Furthermore, even if this were within the scope of the passage, it would be highly unlikely that anyone would think these provisions should be applied to "all possible" situations.*

(E) Copy shops make more of a profit from the preparation and sale of course packs than from other materials.

*SCOPE (out of scope). The passage never discusses profits made from the sale of other materials.*

4. The information in the passage provides the most support for which one of the following statements about copyright law?

(A) Copyright law can be one of the most complex areas of any legal system.

*SCOPE (out of scope). The complexity of other areas of law is not discussed, so no comparison can be made.*

(B) Courts have been inconsistent in their interpretations of certain provisions of copyright law.

*INTERPRETATION (unsupported). The courts disagree with the publishers' argument, and there are hints given that the courts rule differently when different situations arise, but there is no evidence given that they are inconsistent.*

(C) The number of the kinds of materials granted protection under copyright law is steadily decreasing.

*SCOPE (out of scope). This is not mentioned in the passage.*

(D) New practices can compel the courts to refine how copyright law is applied.

*This is the correct answer. The role of copy shops in today's world has compelled the courts to refine their interpretation of the law (lines 18–20).*

(E) Copyright law is primarily concerned with making published materials available for educational use.

*INTERPRETATION (unsupported). Though this specific passage is about copyright law relative to educational use, it is incorrect to assume that copyright law itself is primarily concerned with educational use.*

6

5. Which one of the following describes a role most similar to that of professors in the passage who use copy shops to produce course packs?

(A̶) An artisan generates a legible copy of an old headstone engraving by using charcoal on newsprint and frames and sells high-quality photocopies of it at a crafts market.
   *INTERPRETATION (unsupported). This suggests that we have somehow changed the original item in an artistic fashion, in order to create something new and distinctly different. This is not the case.*

(B) A choir director tapes a selection of another well-known choir's best pieces and sends it to a recording studio to be reproduced in a sellable package for use by members of her choir.
   *This is the correct answer. This is very similar to a professor who picks parts of passages, and sends them out for reproduction and eventual sale to his students.*

(C̶) A grocer makes several kinds of sandwiches that sell for less than similar sandwiches from a nearby upscale cafe.
   *INTERPRETATION (unsupported). This suggests that the copy-shop owners themselves determine what goes into the packs, and make different types, or that the professors themselves are doing the copying, when in fact it is the professors who determine what goes in a course pack and the shop owners do the work of copying. Furthermore, we are not told about the rates of these copy shops relative to their competitors.*

(D̶) A professional graphic artist prints reproductions of several well-known paintings at an exhibit to sell at the museum's gift shop.
   *INTERPRETATION (unsupported). The professors themselves do not make or sell the copies.*

(E̶) A souvenir store in the center of a city sells miniature bronze renditions of a famous bronze sculpture that the city is noted for displaying.
   *INTERPRETATION (unsupported). The professors themselves do not make or sell the copies. Furthermore, the professors themselves have no motivation to make a profit.*

6. Which one of the following, if true, would have most strengthened the publishers' position in this case?

(A̶) Course packs for courses that usually have large enrollments had produced a larger profit for the copy-shop owner.
   *SCOPE (out of scope). The relationship between the size of a course and the size of a copy-shop owner's profits is not discussed in this passage.*

(B̶) The copy-shop owner had actively solicited professors' orders for course packs.
   *SCOPE (out of scope). Whether or not the copy-shop owners solicited professors is not directly or indirectly related to the arguments made in the passage.*

(C̶) The revenue generated by the copy shop's sale of course packs had risen significantly within the past few years.
   *SCOPE (out of scope). This answer compares current profits with past profits. This difference is not relevant to the argument at hand.*

(D) Many area bookstores had reported a marked decrease in the sales of books used for producing course packs.
   *This is the correct answer. It is inferred from elements mentioned directly in the passage: one reason the courts ruled for the shop owners is because they felt that these course packs would not have a detrimental impact on publisher's sales (lines 31–35).*

(E̶) The publishers had enlisted the support of the authors to verify their claims that the copy-shop owner had not obtained permission.
   *SCOPE (out of scope). Whether or not the copy-shop owners obtained permission is not in question.*
   *INTERPRETATION (unsupported). We've already been told that the copy-shop owner acknowledges he did not have permission (line 6).*

6

# Conclusion

## Interpreting Your Results

Determining the reason for an incorrect answer is a subjective enterprise, and it's unnecessary for you to come up with a score for different answer types in this chapter. However, by analyzing incorrect answer types in review, you should be able to fine tune your thought process.

If you are continuing to eliminate answer choices for reasons other than those covered in this chapter, be careful—your reasoning might be strong, but may not be relevant to this exam.

If you are continuing to eliminate answer choices for "vague" reasons, do your best to become as specific as possible. The more specific you can be, the faster you will improve.

6

# Chapter 7

*of*

## Reading Comprehension
### Part 3: *Apply Your Knowledge*

# Comparative Passages

# Comparative Passages

A new trend on the LSAT has been the inclusion, on every test since June 2007, of a set of questions based on two comparative passages written by two different authors.

## Read Like a Judge

Imagine that you are a judge preparing to hear a big case. You have two documents in front of you. You need to make sense of these documents, but you have limited time to review them. To get the most from your read, you would probably consider the following:

**1. How does each document relate *to the central argument* of the case I'm about to hear?**
   • Does it present one side of the argument?
   • Is it just objective background information?
   • Does the author of the document make his or her opinion known?

**2. How do the two documents *relate to each other*?**
   • Do they work with each other or against each other?
   • What common evidence or information is presented across both documents?

This is essentially how you want to view your role as you read comparative passages on the LSAT. The questions will test your ability to understand how each passage relates *to the central argument*, and how the two passages relate *to each other*.

Now, we might anticipate that the two passages will represent the two opposing sides of an argument, but the relationship between comparative passages can often be more complex than that. Let's look at some hypothetical examples to illustrate.

## Examples of Comparative Structures

### EXAMPLE #1

*Passage A*
Argument that on-base percentage (o.b.p.) is a more useful statistic than batting average (b.a.) in determining the success of a baseball player.

Statistical analysis that shows o.b.p. is a better indicator of how many runs that batter will produce for his team.

Evidence that baseball managers routinely place more weight on b.a. than o.b.p. when making determinations about who plays.

*Passage B*
Background information on how on-base percentage is calculated.

Background information on how batting average is calculated.

Historical information about the number of most valuable players who also lead the league in batting average that year.

In this case, the first side of the argument (o.b.p. is a more useful statistic than batting average) allows us to anticipate, or infer, the second side of the argument (batting average is a more useful statistic than o.b.p.), even though it turns out that the second side is never explicitly stated in either passage.

Let's define the central argument in the form of a scale diagram:

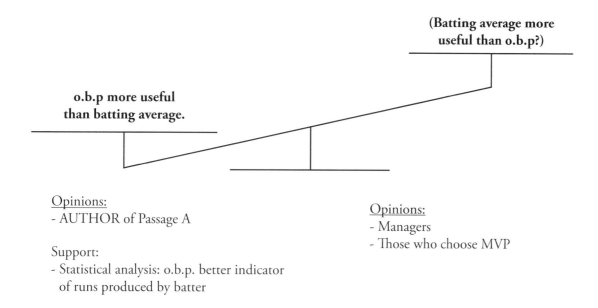

Opinions:
- AUTHOR of Passage A

Support:
- Statistical analysis: o.b.p. better indicator
  of runs produced by batter

Opinions:
- Managers
- Those who choose MVP

Now that we've defined the central argument, and organized the elements of both passages according to this argument, let's consider the all-important questions that we always need to consider when reading comparative passages:

**1. How does each passage relate *to the central argument*?**
Passage A presents one side of the central argument (and allows us to infer the other side). The author of passage A clearly comes down on one side of the argument: o.b.p. is more useful than batting average.

Passage B, on the other hand, does not take sides. Rather, it provides background information to inform the argument.

**2. How do the two passages relate *to each other*?**
Since passage B is relatively neutral in its treatment of this argument, the two passages neither work *with* each other nor work *against* each other.

More important, in this case, is to note the common information or content that is presented across both passages. It is extremely common for Comparative Passage questions to test your ability to see this overlap, or to see where overlap *does not* exist:

*Passage A:*
-**On base percentage**
-**Batting average**
-Statistical analysis
-Baseball managers decision-making process

*Passage B:*
- **on base percentage**
- **batting average**
- MVP history

As an example, consider the following hypothetical question:

> Which of the following is discussed in passage B but not in passage
> A?
>
> (A) on-base percentage
> (B) statistical analysis of on-base percentage as it relates to runs
>     produced
> (C) batting average
> (D) historical relationship between most valuable player awards and
>     batting average
> (E) the factors that baseball managers use to determine which players
>     get playing time

In order to answer this question, we must have a good sense of where the two passages overlap and where they don't. While you don't necessarily have to memorize the overlap on your first read, you should be able to revisit the passages to make a determination.

In this case, the historical relationship between most valuable player awards and batting average is discussed in passage B but not in passage A. Thus, (D) would be the answer.

**EXAMPLE #2**

*Passage A*

Argument that Raymond Carver cannot be considered a significant writer because he derived many of his themes and story lines from the work of Anton Chekhov.

Evidence of several Carver stories that bear similarities to those of Chekhov.

Description of story in which Carver admits he is emulating Chekhov.

*Passage B*

Background information on impact of Carver's work on American literary community.

Argument that Carver's writing is beloved because of his accurate representation of the human condition.

Argument that Carver's work is so significant that it is worthy of being compared to that of Chekhov.

**Carver insignificant
because work is derivative.**

**Carver significant.**

Opinions:
-AUTHOR of passage A

Opinions:
-AUTHOR of passage B

Support:
-Carver stories similar to those of Chekhov
-Carver admits he emulates Chekhov

Support:
-Impact on literary community
-Accurate representation of human condition
-Carver worthy of comparison with Chekhov

**1. How does each passage relate *to the central argument*?**
Passage A defines one side of the argument while passage B defines the other.

**2. How do the two passages relate *to each other*?**
In this case, the two passages come in direct opposition to each other. They definitely work against each other in the sense that they represent opposing sides of the central argument. That said, they do have some common elements.

Let's attempt to define the overlap between the two:

*Passage A:*
-**Carver**
-**Comparison to Chekhov**
-Carver admission of emulation

*Passage B:*
-**Carver**
-Effect on American lit community
-Carver's representation of human condition
-**Comparison to Chekhov**

7

Noteworthy in this case is that both passages acknowledge the similarity between Carver's work and that of Chekhov, but they differ in how they interpret this similarity. Passage A uses the similarity to discredit the work of Carver, whereas passage B uses the similarity as evidence for the significance of Carver's work.

### EXAMPLE #3

*Passage A*
Discussion of the strong correlation between Oscar nominations and box office grosses for films released in the 1960s.

Discussion of the weak correlation between Oscar nominations and box office grosses for films released in the 2000s.

Argument that Oscars are not as relevant as they used to be.

*Passage B*
Background information on the birth of the blockbuster film.

Statistics on financial success of the film *Jaws*.

Analysis of how the blockbuster changed the film industry from one that caters to adults to one that caters to children.

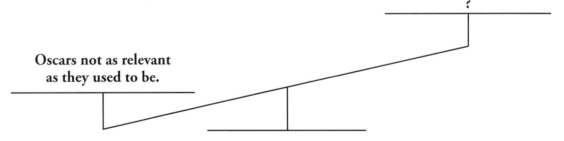

**Oscars not as relevant as they used to be.**

Opinions:
-AUTHOR of Passage A

Support:
-Correlation between Oscar nominations and box office grosses, then and now
-ALL OF PASSAGE B!!

**1. How does each passage relate *to the central* argument?**

Passage A begins with background evidence that supports an argument, and then concludes with that argument, which is that the Oscar is not as relevant as it once was.

Passage B gives an objective history of the blockbuster film. No opinion, no argument.

**2. How do the two passages relate *to each other*?**

In describing how the focus of filmmakers switched from films for adults to films for children, passage B gives a reason for why the argument in passage A might be true. In fact, the entire second passage, though objective in and of itself, could be thought of as evidence that supports the argument made in the first passage!

Notice that there is not much overlap in content between the two passages. Still, the passages are connected through the central argument.

In each of the examples, the two passages are directly or indirectly related to a common argument, but not necessarily opposite sides of that argument. To summarize:

> **Example #1:** Passage A provides one side of an argument while passage B provides neutral background information.
> **Example #2:** Passage A provides one side of an argument while passage B provides the other side.
> **Example #3:** Passage A provides one side of an argument while passage B provides objective historical information that ends up supporting the claim made in passage A.

Be patient as you attempt to figure out exactly what the central argument is. It may not come to you until the middle of the second passage; it may not come to you until after you've read both passages and paused a minute to think about them. Don't rush to judgement; as you read, you should work to understand the relationship between the structure of the argument as a whole and the piece that you are currently reading.

## Timing

Because these questions tend to ask about elements that are potentially mentioned in both passages (the overlap), you are often required to do twice as much work when it comes to verifying your answer choices using the text. Therefore, you want to allot a little extra time for answering the questions.

Ideally, you will read both passages in two to three minutes total, and have five to seven minutes for the questions.

# DRILL IT: Comparative Passages

Do your best to read both passages in a total of three minutes or less. Afterwards, do your best to answer all questions within five minutes total.

### *December 2007, Section 4, Passage 3*

*The passages discuss relationships between business interests and university research.*

### Passage A

As university researchers working in a "gift economy" dedicated to collegial sharing of ideas, we have long been insulated from market pressures. The recent tendency to treat research findings as
(5) commodities, tradable for cash, threatens this tradition and the role of research as a public good.

The nurseries for new ideas are traditionally universities, which provide an environment uniquely suited to the painstaking testing and revision of
(10) theories. Unfortunately, the market process and values governing commodity exchange are ill suited to the cultivation and management of new ideas. With their shareholders impatient for quick returns, businesses are averse to wide-ranging experimentation. And, what
(15) is even more important, few commercial enterprises contain the range of expertise needed to handle the replacement of shattered theoretical frameworks.

Further, since entrepreneurs usually have little affinity for adventure of the intellectual sort, they can
(20) buy research and bury its products, hiding knowledge useful to society or to their competitors. The growth of industrial biotechnology, for example, has been accompanied by a reduction in the free sharing of research methods and results—a high price to pay for
(25) the undoubted benefits of new drugs and therapies.

Important new experimental results once led university scientists to rush down the hall and share their excitement with colleagues. When instead the rush is to patent lawyers and venture capitalists, I
(30) worry about the long-term future of scientific discovery.

### Passage B

The fruits of pure science were once considered primarily a public good, available for society as a whole. The argument for this view was that most of
(35) these benefits were produced through government support of universities, and thus no individual was entitled to restrict access to them.

Today, however, the critical role of science in the modern "information economy" means that what was
(40) previously seen as a public good is being transformed into a market commodity. For example, by exploiting the information that basic research has accumulated about the detailed structures of cells and genes, the biotechnology industry can derive profitable
(45) pharmaceuticals or medical screening technologies. In this context, assertion of legal claims to "intellectual property"—not just in commercial products but in the underlying scientific knowledge—becomes crucial.

Previously, the distinction between a scientific
(50) "discovery" (which could not be patented) and a technical "invention" (which could) defined the limits of industry's ability to patent something. Today, however, the speed with which scientific discoveries can be turned into products and the large profits
(55) resulting from this transformation have led to a blurring of both the legal distinction between discovery and invention and the moral distinction between what should and should not be patented.

Industry argues that if it had supported—either in
(60) its own laboratories or in a university—the makers of a scientific discovery, then it is entitled to seek a return on its investment, either by charging others for using the discovery or by keeping it for its own exclusive use.

15. Which one of the following is discussed in passage B but not in passage A?

(A) the blurring of the legal distinction between discovery and invention

(B) the general effects of the market on the exchange of scientific knowledge

(C) the role of scientific research in supplying public goods

(D) new pharmaceuticals that result from industrial research

(E) industry's practice of restricting access to research findings

16. Both passages place in opposition the members of which one of the following pairs?

(A) commercially successful research and commercially unsuccessful research

(B) research methods and research results

(C) a marketable commodity and a public good

(D) a discovery and an invention

(E) scientific research and other types of inquiry

17. Both passages refer to which one of the following?

(A)  theoretical frameworks
(B)  venture capitalists
(C)  physics and chemistry
(D)  industrial biotechnology
(E)  shareholders

18. It can be inferred from the passages that the authors believe that the increased constraint on access to scientific information and ideas arises from

(A)  the enormous increase in the volume of scientific knowledge that is being generated
(B)  the desire of individual researchers to receive credit for their discoveries
(C)  the striving of commercial enterprises to gain a competitive advantage in the market
(D)  moral reservations about the social impact of some scientific research
(E)  a drastic reduction in government funding for university research

19. Which one of the following statements is most strongly supported by both passages?

(A)  Many scientific researchers who previously worked in universities have begun to work in the biotechnology industry.
(B)  Private biotechnology companies have invalidly patented the basic research findings of university researchers.
(C)  Because of the nature of current scientific research, patent authorities no longer consider the distinction between discoveries and inventions to be clear cut.
(D)  In the past, scientists working in industry had free access to the results of basic research conducted in universities.
(E)  Government-funded research in universities has traditionally been motivated by the goals of private industry.

7

# SOLUTIONS: Comparative Passages

As we read the passages, we'll take on the perspective of a judge looking for the central argument, the sides of this argument, and the evidence used to support either side of the argument. Because this is an example of comparative passages, we'll pay particular attention to (1) how each passage relates to the central argument, and (2) how the two passages relate to each other. Below is a real-time analysis of the passage, including annotations. Notice how the reader's understanding of the passages evolves throughout the process.

### December 2007, Section 4, Passage 3

*The passages discuss relationships between business interests and university research.*

**Passage A**
As university researchers working in a "gift economy" dedicated to collegial sharing of ideas, we have long been insulated from market pressures. <u>The recent tendency to treat research findings as commodities, tradable for cash, threatens this tradition and the role of research as a public good.</u>

*Strong statement right from the start. This looks like it could be one side of an argument. We'll guess the other side: that treating research findings as tradable commodities actually strengthens the role of research as a public good. We'll see though...*

Research for money threatens role of research as a public good.

(Research for money *strengthens* role of research as a public good??)

Opinions:
AUTHOR (A)

The nurseries for new ideas are traditionally universities, which provide an environment uniquely suited to the painstaking testing and revision of theories. Unfortunately, the market process and values governing commodity exchange are ill suited to the cultivation and management of new ideas. With their shareholders impatient for quick returns, businesses are averse to wide-ranging experimentation. And, what is even more important, few commercial enterprises contain the range of expertise needed to handle the replacement of shattered theoretical frameworks.

*This paragrah is a mix of background information and support for the left side of the scale. Still no word on the right side of the scale. Not sure if our guess is completely correct yet.*

Research for money threatens role of research as a public good.

(Research for money *strengthens* role of research as a public good??)

Opinions:
AUTHOR (A)

Support for:
-Open market ill suited
-Commercial enterprises lack expertise

Further, since entrepreneurs usually have little affinity for adventure of the intellectual sort, they can buy research and bury its products, hiding knowledge useful to society or to their competitors. The growth of industrial biotechnology, for example, has been accompanied by a reduction in the free sharing of research methods and results—a high price to pay for the undoubted benefits of new drugs and therapies.

*More evidence to support the left side.*

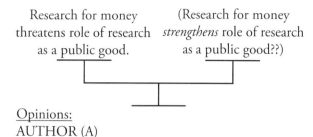

Research for money threatens role of research as <u>a public good</u>.

(Research for money *strengthens* role of research as <u>a public good</u>??)

<u>Opinions:</u>
AUTHOR (A)

<u>Support for:</u>
-Open market ill suited
-Commercial enterprises lack expertise
-Entrepreneurs hide knowledge (e.g., biotechnology)

Important new experimental results once led university scientists to rush down the hall and share their excitement with colleagues. <u>When instead the rush is to patent lawyers and venture capitalists, I worry about the long-term future of scientific discovery.</u>

(A)

*A reiteration of the author's opinion. This doesn't change our understanding at all. So far we have one side of an argument, and a guess at what the other side might be. Let's see what passage B holds.*

7

**Passage B**

The fruits of pure science were once considered primarily a public good, available for society as a whole. The argument for this view was that most of these benefits were produced through government support of universities, and thus no individual was entitled to restrict access to them.

Today, however, the critical role of science in the modern "information economy" means that what was previously seen as a public good is being transformed into a market commodity. For example, by exploiting the information that basic research has accumulated about the detailed structures of cells and genes, the biotechnology industry can derive profitable pharmaceuticals or medical screening technologies. In this context, assertion of legal claims to "intellectual property"—not just in commercial products but in the underlying scientific knowledge—becomes crucial.

Previously, the distinction between a scientific "discovery" (which could not be patented) and a technical "invention" (which could) defined the limits of industry's ability to patent something. Today, however, the speed with which scientific discoveries can be turned into products and the large profits resulting from this transformation have led to a blurring of both the legal distinction between discovery and invention and the moral distinction between what should and should not be patented.

Industry argues that if it had supported—either in its own laboratories or in a university—the makers of a scientific discovery, then it is entitled to seek a return on its investment, either by charging others for using the discovery or by keeping it for its own exclusive use.

*This entire passage seems like background information. The tone is much more objective and factual in nature, simply documenting a trend in the treatment of scientific findings.*

*While the opinion of this author is difficult to discern, he or she obviously believes that that there has been a trend away from science as a public good and towards science as a marketable commodity.*

*Thus, we're left with this as our final understanding (the right side was never really fleshed out):*

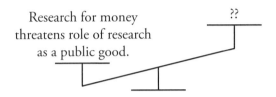

Research for money threatens role of research as a public good.

Opinions:
AUTHOR (A)

Support for:
-Open market ill suited
-Commercial enterprises lack expertise
-Entrepreneurs hide knowledge (e.g., biotechnology)

**1. How does each passage relate to the central argument?**

Passage A clearly defines one side of the central argument, whereas passage B simply provides background information.

**2. How do the two passages relate to each other?**

Passage A makes an argument, and passage B gives mostly objective information that seems to inform that argument.

Note that *all five* of these questions test your ability to see the overlap, or the lack of overlap, across passages. In other words, they test your ability to *relate the two passages to each other*.

You shouldn't try to memorize the overlapping components as you read. Rather, simply attempt to notice the topics and examples that are used across both passages. When it comes time to answer the questions, you should refer back to the passages to confirm your answer.

15. Which one of the following is discussed in passage B but not in passage A?

(A)  the blurring of the legal distinction between discovery and invention
(B)  the general effects of the market on the exchange of scientific knowledge
(C)  the role of scientific research in supplying public goods
(D)  new pharmaceuticals that result from industrial research
(E)  industry's practice of restricting access to research findings

*(A)* **CORRECT.** *The legal distinction between "discovery and invention" is discussed in passage B but not in passage A.*

*(B) Passage A discusses "research findings as commodities" as a threat, and passage B highlights a trend towards research findings as "market commodities."*

*(C) Both passages discuss scientific research as a public good.*

*(D) Passage A discusses "new drugs and therapies," while passage B mentions "pharmaceuticals" resulting from industrial biotechnology.*

*(E) Passage A mentions that entrepreneurs "buy research and bury its products," while passage B discusses industry's right to keep discoveries "for its own exclusive use."*

16. Both passages place in opposition the members of which one of the following pairs?

(A)  commercially successful research and commercially unsuccessful research
(B)  research methods and research results
(C)  a marketable commodity and a public good
(D)  a discovery and an invention
(E)  scientific research and other types of inquiry

*(A) Both passages mention industrial biotechnology, but neither passage compares commercially successful endeavors with commercially unsuccessful endeavors.*

*(B) Specific research methods are not discussed in either passage.*

*(C)* **CORRECT.** *Both passages discuss the trend away from research as a public good and towards research as a market commodity.*

*(D) The legal distinction between discoveries and inventions is discussed in passage B but not in passage A.*

*(E) Scientific research is discussed in both passages, but other types of inquiry are not discussed in either passage.*

7

17. Both passages refer to which one of the following?

(A) theoretical frameworks
(B) venture capitalists
(C) physics and chemistry
(D) industrial biotechnology
(E) shareholders

*(A) Passage A discusses industry's inability to deal with "shattered theoretical frameworks," but passage B never discusses theoretical frameworks.*

*(B) Passage A discusses the new trend towards sharing research findings with "patent lawyers and venture capitalists," but passage B never mentions venture capitalists.*

*(C) While biotechnology is mentioned in both passages, physics and chemistry specifically are never discussed.*

*(D) **CORRECT.** Both passages specifically refer to biotechnology.*

*(E) Passage A mentions "shareholders impatient for quick returns," but passage B never mentions shareholders.*

18. It can be inferred from the passages that the authors believe that the increased constraint on access to scientific information and ideas arises from

(A) the enormous increase in the volume of scientific knowledge that is being generated
(B) the desire of individual researchers to receive credit for their discoveries
(C) the striving of commercial enterprises to gain a competitive advantage in the market
(D) moral reservations about the social impact of some scientific research
(E) a drastic reduction in government funding for university research

*(A) The volume of scientific knowledge is not discussed in either passage.*

*(B) The desires of individual researchers are not discussed in either passage.*

*(C) **CORRECT.** Passage A discusses an entrepreneur's ability to "hide knowledge useful to society or its competitors," presumably to gain a competitive advantage. Passage B discusses industry's inclination to keep discoveries for "its own exclusive use."*

*(D) Watch out! Passage B discusses a "moral distinction between what should and should not be patented," but NOT "moral reservations about the social impact of scientific research."*

*(E) Reductions in government funding are not discussed in either passage.*

19. Which one of the following statements is most strongly supported by both passages?

(A) Many scientific researchers who previously worked in universities have begun to work in the biotechnology industry.

(B) Private biotechnology companies have invalidly patented the basic research findings of university researchers.

(C) Because of the nature of current scientific research, patent authorities no longer consider the distinction between discoveries and inventions to be clear cut.

(D) In the past, scientists working in industry had free access to the results of basic research conducted in universities.

(E) Government-funded research in universities has traditionally been motivated by the goals of private industry.

*(A) Though this would flow logically with some of the items mentioned in the passages, there is no direct reference made to researchers switching jobs.*

*(B) Neither passage discusses any biotech companies that have invalidly patented research findings.*

*(C) Passage B discusses the "blurring of both the legal distinction between discovery and invention and the moral distinction between what should and should not be patented," but passage A never mentions the distinction between discovery and invention.*

*(D) **CORRECT**. This free access is mentioned throughout passage A and in the first paragraph of passage B.*

*(E) The motivations of government-funded research are not discussed in either passage.*

7

# Conclusion

**1. Read like a judge.** Both passages will be directly or indirectly related to a central argument, but will not necessarily represent opposing sides of that argument.

**2. Relate to the argument, relate to each other.** During the reading process, it is important to note (1) how each passage relates to the central argument, and (2) how the passages relate to each other.

**3. Note passage overlap.** Most questions hinge on your understanding of the similarities and differences between the passages. Do not assume that your memory of what you saw on your first read is "enough." Confirm your answer by rereading the relevant parts of both passages.

**4. Leave enough time.** It is important to allocate enough time to verify each correct answer carefully. If possible, you need to finish the reading process quickly to have the time to properly answer the questions.

**7**

# Chapter 8
## of
## Reading Comprehension

# Putting It All Together

# The Complete Process

Let's review some general information, tips, and strategies that pertain to timing, reading the passage, and answering the questions.

<table>
<tr><td align="center">TIMING</td></tr>
</table>

- You have 35 minutes for the section, which averages out to 8:45 per passage.
- You will want to spend less time on easier passages in order to devote more time to harder passages.
- However, you need to adjust your timing based on the particular exam. If passage 1 is very difficult to understand, give yourself some extra time to read it (chances are some of the other passages will be easier to understand than normal). If passage 3 seems easy to understand, push through it quickly, because chances are passage 4 will make up for it by being especially challenging.
- In general, you want to spend more time answering questions than reading the text. Again, continue to adjust your allocation based on the characteristics of the particular exam, and based on your own strengths and weaknesses.

<table>
<tr><td align="center">THE READING PROCESS</td></tr>
</table>

- Most passages are directly or indirectly related to a central argument.
- Some passages discuss both sides of the argument.
- Others use the argument only as a starting point for a discussion of one side.
- In either case, you can use the image of a scale to mentally organize the rest of the text.
- Relative to the central argument, other parts of the passage can be assigned roles such as background information, opinions for one side or the other, or supporting evidence for one side or the other.
- Notate the elements of the passage that describe the central argument, or have information about opinions, particularly the author's opinion.
- Mentally organize and assign roles to the parts of the text you don't annotate.
- Don't get lost in the nuances and details of a supporting piece of text as long as you understand the role it plays.
- Push the pace in order to spend as much time answering the questions as possible.

<table>
<tr><td align="center">ANSWERING THE QUESTIONS</td></tr>
</table>

- Use both the prompt and the answer choices to get a sense of the types of mental processes (identification, inference, or synthesis) that the question requires.
- Take the extra time needed to carefully read and completely understand long or complicated prompts, especially those that involve double negatives.
- Go through two rounds of elimination.
- Get rid of obviously wrong answers first by using your understanding of incorrect answer characteristics (interpretation, scope, degree).
- Devote extra time to carefully evaluating the remaining choices.
- Don't eliminate answer choices until you are certain they are wrong.
- Be wary of answers that stray too far from the text, or require too big a logic leap.
- Whenever possible, confirm your answer by rereading the text.

**8**

## Are You Correctly Aligned?

Let's go back to the self-assessment chart we introduced in Chapter 1. Read through it carefully, and see if there are any last-minute adjustments you want to make.

| SIGNS THAT YOU ARE SPEND-ING TOO LITTLE TIME IN THE READING PROCESS | SIGNS THAT YOU ARE SPEND-ING TOO MUCH TIME IN THE READING PROCESS |
|---|---|
| You have trouble recognizing the central argument. <br><br> You have trouble organizing the information in the passage relative to the argument. <br><br> You don't understand the role each paragraph plays relative to the rest of the passage. <br><br> You have trouble paraphrasing the purpose of a paragraph. <br><br> You don't have a clear sense of the author's opinion. <br><br> You don't have a clear sense of which opinions contrast one another. <br><br> You often miss problems pertaining to the passage as a whole. <br><br> You often have to go back and reread the text in order to answer questions about the passage as a whole. <br><br> You do poorly on questions that ask you to compare the text to some sort of analogy. <br><br> You often feel lost when you have to go back into the text to find answers to questions that ask about a specific detail. | You try to memorize and notate every single detail in the text. <br><br> While you are reading, you try to go beyond understanding the text relative to the central argument and try to see what else you can infer. <br><br> You spend a lot of extra time trying to understand specific elements of the text, elements that ultimately don't show up in the questions. <br><br> You feel rushed while going through the questions. <br><br> You often feel that you do not have time to go through the process of elimination. <br><br> You often answer off of a "gut" feeling. <br><br> You often feel you do not have enough time to return to the text in order to verify the answer to a specific question. |

8

# Are We There Yet?

Let's take a final look at the common characteristics of those who perform exceptionally well on the LSAT. Do one final assessment: in what areas do you fall on the left side of the chart, and in what areas do you fall on the right?

You certainly don't have to fall on the left side for every category; everyone has a different style that is most effective for him or her. However, for all the areas that you do fall on the right side of the chart, you want to ask yourself, "Does this in some way hinder my ability to answer questions accurately and efficiently?" If so, you want to work to address the issue.

| 170+ | Average Test-Taker |
|---|---|
| Is able to mentally organize the passage as she reads. | Reads passively and absorbs information in an unorganized manner. |
| Uses paragraphs as organizational tools. | Jumps from paragraph to paragraph without pausing and reflecting. |
| Upon reflection, can easily assign roles for each part of the passage. | Does not have a clear understanding of how the different parts of the passage relate to one another. |
| Takes the time to carefully understand confusing question prompts. | Rushes through confusing question prompts and answers without a clear sense of the question. |
| Starts problems by actively seeking to eliminate wrong answers. | Starts by looking for the right answer. |
| Uses an understanding of incorrect answer characteristics to confidently eliminate obviously incorrect answers. | Uses instinct, or "gut sense," to evaluate answers. |
| Rarely returns to an answer that he or she eliminates. | Eliminates some answers with certainty and some without, and often has to go back and reexamine every answer choice again. |
| Spends the majority of his or her time breaking down and double-checking the most attractive answer choices. | Wastes time overthinking obviously incorrect choices, and doesn't have time to carefully examine the most likely possibilities. |

# The Final Drill

Congratulations! You are almost done! Here is one final drill you can use to incorporate all of the different lessons we've discussed.

On the following pages is a complete Reading Comprehension section from a past LSAT exam (June 2003). This should be a good representation of what you will experience on test day (the only difference is that this drill does not contain comparative passages, whereas your test will include one set of comparative passages).

Complete the drill as if you were in the actual exam. Give yourself 35 minutes, keep track of the time you spend reading each passage and answering each set of questions, and don't take any breaks!

Following the drill are two explanations: The 180 Experience and Detailed Explanations.

The point of the drill is *not* to see if your thought processes fit exactly into some set form. Different 180 test-takers will read the passages in different ways, and assigning reasons for incorrect answers is a highly subjective art form.

Rather, use the drill and the explanations to reflect on your own testing experience. See if there are some general, fundamental flaws in the way you are taking the exam. Perhaps you are spending too much time reading the text initially; perhaps you are often tricked by one particular type of incorrect answer choice. Use the explanations to evaluate your own general tendencies and to identify areas for improvement.

8

**June 2003, Section 4**

27 Questions, 35 minutes

<u>Directions:</u> Each passage in this section is followed by a group of questions to be answered on the basis of what is <u>stated</u> or implied in the passage. For some of the questions, more than one of the choices could conceivably answer the question. However, you are to choose the <u>best</u> answer; that is, the response that most accurately and completely answers the question, and blacken the corresponding space on your answer sheet.

Social scientists have traditionally defined multipolar international systems as consisting of three or more nations, each of roughly equal military and economic strength. Theoretically, the members of such
(5) systems create shifting, temporary alliances in response to changing circumstances in the international environment. Such systems are, thus, fluid and flexible. Frequent, small confrontations are one attribute of multipolar systems and are usually the result of less
(10) powerful members grouping together to counter threats from larger, more aggressive members seeking hegemony. Yet the constant and inevitable counterbalancing typical of such systems usually results in stability. The best-known example of a
(15) multipolar system is the Concert of Europe, which coincided with general peace on that continent lasting roughly 100 years beginning around 1815.

Bipolar systems, on the other hand, involve two major members of roughly equal military and
(20) economic strength vying for power and advantage. Other members of lesser strength tend to coalesce around one or the other pole. Such systems tend to be rigid and fixed, in part due to the existence of only one axis of power. Zero-sum political and military
(25) maneuverings, in which a gain for one side results in an equivalent loss for the other, are a salient feature of bipolar systems. Overall superiority is sought by both major members which can lead to frequent confrontations, debilitating armed conflict, and,
(30) eventually, to the capitulation of one or the other side. Athens and Sparta of ancient Greece had a bipolar relationship, as did the United States and the USSR during the Cold War.

However, the shift in the geopolitical landscape
(35) following the end of the Cold War calls for a reassessment of the assumptions underlying these two theoretical concepts. The emerging but still vague multipolar system in Europe today brings with it the unsettling prospect of new conflicts and shifting
(40) alliances that may lead to a diminution, rather than an enhancement, of security. The frequent, small confrontations that are thought to have kept the Concert of Europe in a state of equilibrium would today, as nations arm themselves with modern
(45) weapons, create instability that could destroy the system. And the larger number of members and shifting alliance patterns peculiar to multipolar systems

would create a bewildering tangle of conflicts.

This reassessment may also lead us to look at the
(50) Cold War in a new light. In 1914 smaller members of the multipolar system in Europe brought the larger members into a war that engulfed the continent. The aftermath—a crippled system in which certain members were dismantled, punished, or voluntarily
(55) withdrew—created the conditions that led to World War II. In contrast, the principal attributes of bipolar systems—two major members with only one possible axis of conflict locked in a rigid yet usually stable struggle for power—may have created the necessary
(60) parameters for general peace in the second half of the twentieth century.

1. Which one of the following most accurately expresses the main point of the passage?

(A) Peace can be maintained in Europe only if a new bipolar system emerges to replace Cold War alliances.

(B) All kinds of international systems discussed by social scientists carry within themselves the seeds of their own collapse and ultimately endanger international order.

(C) The current European geopolitical landscape is a multipolar system that strongly resembles the Concert of Europe which existed through most of the nineteenth century.

(D) Multipolarity fostered the conditions that led to World War II and is incompatible with a stable, modern Europe.

(E) The characterization of multipolar systems as stable and bipolar systems as open to debilitating conflict needs to be reconsidered in light of the realities of post-Cold War Europe.

2. Which one of the following statements most accurately describes the function of the final paragraph?

(A) The weaknesses of both types of systems are discussed in the context of twentieth-century European history.

(B) A prediction is made regarding European security based on the attributes of both types of systems.

(C) A new argument is introduced in favor of European countries embracing a new bipolar system.

(D) Twentieth-century European history is used to expand on the argument in the previous paragraph.

(E) The typical characteristics of the major members of a bipolar system are reviewed.

3. The author's reference to the possibility that confrontations may lead to capitulation (lines 27–30) serves primarily to

(A) indicate that bipolar systems can have certain unstable characteristics

(B) illustrate how multipolar systems can transform themselves into bipolar systems

(C) contrast the aggressive nature of bipolar members with the more rational behavior of their multipolar counterparts

(D) indicate the anarchic nature of international relations

(E) suggest that military and economic strength shifts in bipolar as frequently as in multipolar systems

4. With respect to the Cold War, the author's attitude can most accurately be described as

(A) fearful that European geopolitics may bring about a similar bipolar system

(B) surprised that it did not end with a major war

(C) convinced that it provides an important example of bipolarity maintaining peace

(D) regretful that the major European countries were so ambivalent about it

(E) confident it will mark only a brief hiatus between long periods of European multipolarity

5. Which one of the following statements concerning the Concert of Europe (lines 14–17) can most reasonably be inferred from the passage?

(A) Each of the many small confrontations that occurred under the Concert of Europe threatened the integrity of the system.

(B) It provided the highest level of security possible for Europe in the late nineteenth century.

(C) All the factors contributing to stability during the late nineteenth century continue to contribute to European security.

(D) Equilibrium in the system was maintained as members grouped together to counterbalance mutual threats.

(E) It was more stable than most multipolar systems because its smaller members reacted promptly to aggression by its larger members.

8

In spite of a shared language, Latin American poetry written in Spanish differs from Spanish poetry in many respects. The Spanish of Latin American poets is more open than that of Spanish poets, more exposed
(5) to outside influences—indigenous, English, French, and other languages. While some literary critics maintain that there is as much linguistic unity in Latin American poetry as there is in Spanish poetry, they base this claim on the fact that Castilian Spanish, the
(10) official and literary version of the Spanish language based largely on the dialect originally spoken in the Castile region of Spain, was transplanted to the Americas when it was already a relatively standardized idiom. Although such unity may have characterized the
(15) earliest Latin American poetry, after centuries in the Americas the language of Lain American poetry cannot help but reveal the influences of its unique cultural history.

Latin American poetry is critical or irreverent in its
(20) attitude toward language, where that of Spanish poets is more accepting. For example, the Spanish-language incarnations of modernism and the avant-garde, two literary movements that used language in innovative and challenging ways, originated with Latin American
(25) poets. By contrast, when these movements later reached Spain, Spanish poets greeted them with reluctance. Spanish poets, even those of the modern era, seem to take their language for granted, rarely using it in radical or experimental ways.

(30)    The most distinctive note in Latin American poetry is its enthusiastic response to the modern world, while Spanish poetry displays a kind of cultural conservatism—the desire to return to an ideal culture of the distant past. Because no Spanish-language
(35) culture lies in the equally distant (i.e., pre-Columbian) past of the Americas, but has instead been invented by Latin Americans day by day, Latin American poetry has no such long-standing past to romanticize. Instead, Latin American poetry often displays a curiosity about
(40) the literature of other cultures, an interest in exploring poetic structures beyond those typical of Spanish poetry. For example, the first Spanish-language haiku—a Japanese poetic form—were written by José Juan Tablada, a Mexican. Another of the Latin
(45) American poets' responses to this absence is the search for a world before recorded history—not only that of Spain or the Americas, but in some cases of the planet; the Chilean poet Pablo Neruda's work, for example, is noteworthy for its development of an ahistorical
(50) mythology for the creation of the earth. For Latin American poets there is no such thing as the pristine cultural past affirmed in the poetry of Spain: there is only the fluid interaction of all world cultures, or else the extensive time before cultures began.

6. The discussion in the second paragraph is intended primarily to

(A) argue that Latin American poets originated modernism and the avant-garde

(B) explain how Spanish poetry and Latin American poetry differ in their attitudes toward the Spanish language

(C) demonstrate why Latin American poetry is not well received in Spain

(D) show that the Castilian Spanish employed in Spanish poetry has remained relatively unchanged by the advent of modernism and the avant-garde

(E) illustrate the extent to which Spanish poetry romanticizes Spanish-language culture

7. Given the information in the passage, which one of the following is most analogous to the evolution of Latin American poetry?

(A) A family moves its restaurant to a new town and incorporates local ingredients into its traditional recipes.

(B) A family moves its business to a new town after the business fails in its original location.

(C) A family with a two-hundred-year-old house labors industriously in order to restore the house to its original appearance.

(D) A family does research into its ancestry in order to construct its family tree.

(E) A family eagerly anticipates its annual vacation but never takes photographs or purchases souvenirs to preserve its memories.

8. The passage's claims about Spanish poetry would be most weakened if new evidence indicating which one of the following were discovered?

(A) Spanish linguistic constructs had greater influence on Latin American poets than had previously been thought.

(B) Castilian Spanish was still evolving linguistically at the time of the inception of Latin American poetry.

(C) Spanish poets originated an influential literary movement that used language in radical ways.

(D) Castilian Spanish was influenced during its evolution by other Spanish dialects.

(E) Spanish poets rejected the English and French incarnations of modernism.

8

9. The passage affirms each of the following EXCEPT:

(A)  The first haiku in the Spanish language were written by a Latin American poet.

(B)  Spanish poetry is rarely innovative or experimental in its use of language.

(C)  Spanish poetry rarely incorporates poetic traditions from other cultures.

(D)  Latin American poetry tends to take the Spanish language for granted.

(E)  Latin American poetry incorporates aspects of various other languages.

10. Which one of the following can most reasonably be inferred from the passage about Latin American poetry's use of poetic structures from other world cultures?

(A)  The use of poetic structures from other world cultures is an attempt by Latin American poets to create a cultural past.

(B)  The use of poetic structures from other world cultures by Latin American poets is a response to their lack of a long-standing Spanish-language cultural past in the Americas.

(C)  The use of poetic structures from other world cultures has led Latin American poets to reconsider their lack of a long-standing Spanish-language cultural past in the Americas.

(D)  Latin American poets who write about a world before recorded history do not use poetic structures from other world cultures.

(E)  Latin American poetry does not borrow poetic structures from other world cultures whose literature exhibits cultural conservatism.

11. Based on the passage, the author most likely holds which one of the following views toward Spanish poetry's relationship to the Spanish cultural past?

(A)  This relationship has inspired Spanish poets to examine their cultural past with a critical eye.

(B)  This relationship forces Spanish poets to write about subjects with which they feel little natural affinity.

(C)  This relationship is itself the central theme of much Spanish poetry.

(D)  This relationship infuses Spanish poetry with a romanticism that is reluctant to embrace the modern era.

(E)  This relationship results in poems that are of little interest to contemporary Spanish readers.

12. Which one of the following inferences is most supported by the passage?

(A)  A tradition of cultural conservatism has allowed the Spanish language to evolve into a stable, reliable form of expression.

(B)  It was only recently that Latin American poetry began to incorporate elements of other languages.

(C)  The cultural conservatism of Spanish poetry is exemplified by the uncritical attitude of Spanish poets toward the Spanish language.

(D)  Lain American poets' interest in other world cultures is illustrated by their use of Japanese words and phrases.

(E)  Spanish poetry is receptive to the influence of some Spanish-language poets outside of Spain.

8

According the the theory of gravitation, every
particle of matter in the universe attracts every other
particle with a force that increases as either the mass of
the particle increase, or their proximity to one
(5) another increases, or both. Gravitation is believed to
shape the structures of stars, galaxies, and the entire
universe. But for decades cosmologists (scientists who
study the universe) have attempted to account for the
finding that at least 90 percent of the universe seems to
(10) be missing: that the total amount of observable
matter—stars, dust, and miscellaneous debris—does
not contain enough mass to explain why the universe is
organized in the shape of galaxies and clusters of
galaxies. To account for this discrepancy, cosmologists
(15) hypothesize that something else, which they call "dark
matter," provides the gravitational force necessary to
make the huge structures cohere.

What is dark matter? Numerous exotic entities
have been postulated, but among the more attractive
(20) candidates—because they are known actually to
exist—are neutrinos, elementary particles created as a
by-product of nuclear fusion, radioactive decay, or
catastrophic collisions between other particles.
Neutrinos, which come in three types, are by far the
(25) most numerous kind of particle in the universe;
however, they have long been assumed to have no
mass. If so, that would disqualify them as dark matter.
Without mass, matter cannot exert gravitational force;
without such force, it cannot induce other matter to
(30) cohere.

But new evidence suggests that a neutrino does
have mass. This evidence came by way of research
findings supporting the existence of a long-theorized
but never observed phenomenon called oscillation,
(35) whereby each of the three neutrino types can change
into one of the others as it travels through space.
Researchers held that the transformation is possible
only if neutrinos also have mass. They obtained
experimental confirmation of the theory by generating
(40) one neutrino type and then finding evidence that it had
oscillated into the predicted neutrino type. In the
process, they were able to estimate the mass of a
neutrino at from 0.5 to 5 electron volts.

While slight, even the lowest estimate would yield
(45) a lot of mass given that neutrinos are so numerous,
especially considering that neutrinos were previously
assumed to have no mass. Still, even at the highest
estimate, neutrinos could only account for about
20 percent of the universe's "missing" mass.
(50) Nevertheless, that is enough to alter our picture of the
universe even if it does not account for all of dark
matter. In fact, some cosmologists claim that this new
evidence offers the best theoretical solution yet to the
dark matter problem. If the evidence holds up, these
(55) cosmologists believe, it may add to our understanding
of the role elementary particles play in holding the
universe together.

13. Which one of the following most accurately
expresses the main idea of the passage?

(A) Although cosmologists believe that the universe
is shaped by gravitation, the total amount of
observable matter in the universe is greatly
insufficient to account for the gravitation that
would be required to cause the universe to be
organized into galaxies.

(B) Given their inability to account for more than 20
percent of the universe's "missing" mass, scientists
are beginning to speculate that our current
understanding of gravity is significantly mistaken.

(C) Indirect evidence suggesting that neutrinos have
mass may allow neutrinos to account for up to
20 percent of dark matter, a finding that could
someday be extended to a complete solution of the
dark matter problem.

(D) After much speculation, researchers have
discovered that neutrinos oscillate from one
type into another as they travel through space,
a phenomenon that proves that neutrinos have
mass.

(E) Although it has been established that neutrinos
have mass, such mass does not support the
speculation of cosmologists that neutrinos
constitute a portion of the universe's "missing"
mass.

14. Which one of the following titles most completely
and accurately expresses the contents of the passage?

(A) "The Existence of Dark Matter: Arguments For
and Against"

(B) "Neutrinos and the Dark Matter Problem: A
Partial Solution?"

(C) "Too Little, Too Late: Why Neutrinos Do Not
Constitute Dark Matter"

(D) "The Role of Gravity: How Dark Matter Shapes
Stars"

(E) "The Implications of Oscillation: Do Neutrinos
Really Have Mass?"

15. Based on the passage, the author most likely holds which one of the following views?

(A) Observable matter constitutes at least 90 percent of the mass of the universe.
(B) Current theories are incapable of identifying the force that causes all particles in the universe to attract one another.
(C) The key to the problem of dark matter is determining the exact mass of a neutrino.
(D) It is unlikely that any force other than gravitation will be required to account for the organization of the universe into galaxies.
(E) Neutrinos probably account for most of the universe's "missing" mass.

16. As described in the last paragraph of the passage, the cosmologists' approach to solving the dark matter problem is most analogous to which one of the following?

(A) A child seeking information about how to play chess consults a family member and so learns of a book that will instruct her in the game.
(B) A child seeking to earn money by delivering papers is unable to earn enough money for a bicycle and so decides to buy a skateboard instead.
(C) A child hoping to get a dog for his birthday is initially disappointed when his parents bring home a cat but eventually learns to love the animal.
(D) A child seeking money to attend a movie is given some of the money by one of his siblings and so decides to go to each of his other siblings to ask for additional money.
(E) A child enjoys playing sports with the neighborhood children but her parents insist that she cannot participate until she has completed her household chores.

17. The author's attitude towards oscillation can most accurately be characterized as being

(A) satisfied that it occurs and that it suggests that neutrinos have mass
(B) hopeful that it will be useful in discovering other forms of dark matter
(C) concerned that it is often misinterpreted to mean that neutrinos account for all of dark matter
(D) skeptical that it occurs until further research can be done
(E) convinced that it cannot occur outside an experimental setting

18. Which one of the following phrases could replace the world "cohere" at line 30 without substantively altering the author's meaning?

(A) exert gravitational force
(B) form galactic structures
(C) oscillate into another type of matter
(D) become significantly more massive
(E) fuse to produce new particles

19. The passage states each of the following EXCEPT:

(A) There are more neutrinos in the universe than there are non-neutrinos.
(B) Observable matter cannot exert enough gravitational force to account for the present structure of the universe.
(C) Scientific experiments support the theory of neutrino oscillation.
(D) Neutrinos likely cannot account for all of the universe's "missing" mass.
(E) Dark matter may account for a large portion of the universe's gravitational force.

8

Leading questions—questions worded in such a way as to suggest a particular answer—can yield unreliable testimony either by design, as when a lawyer tries to trick a witness into affirming a particular
(5) version of the evidence of a case, or by accident, when a questioner unintentionally prejudices the witness's response. For this reason, a judge can disallow such questions in the courtroom interrogation of witnesses. But their exclusion from the courtroom by no means
(10) eliminates the remote effects of earlier leading questions on eyewitness testimony. Alarmingly, the beliefs about an event that a witness brings to the courtroom may often be adulterated by the effects of leading questions that were introduced intentionally or
(15) unintentionally by lawyers, police investigators, reporters, or others with whom the witness has already interacted.

Recent studies have confirmed the ability of leading questions to alter the details of our memories
(20) and have led to a better understanding of how this process occurs and, perhaps, of the conditions that make for greater risks that an eyewitness's memories have been tainted by leading questions. These studies suggest that not all details of our experiences become
(25) clearly or stably stored in memory—only those to which we give adequate attention. Moreover, experimental evidence indicates that if subtly introduced new data involving remembered events do not actively conflict with our stored memory data, we
(30) tend to process such new data similarly whether they correspond to details as we remember them, or to gaps in those details. In the former case, we often retain the new data as a reinforcement of the corresponding aspect of the memory, and in the latter case, we often
(35) retain them as a construction to fill the corresponding gap. An eyewitness who is asked, prior to courtroom testimony, "How fast was the car going when it passed the stop sign?" may respond to the query about speed without addressing the question of the stop sign. But
(40) the "stop sign" datum has now been introduced, and when later recalled, perhaps during courtroom testimony, it may be processed as belonging to the original memory even if the witness actually saw no stop sign.
(45)     The farther removed from the event, the greater the chance of a vague or incomplete recollection and the greater the likelihood of newly suggested information blending with original memories. Since we can be more easily misled with respect to fainter and more
(50) uncertain memories, tangential details are more apt to become constructed out of subsequently introduced information than are more central details. But what is tangential to a witness's original experience of an event may nevertheless be crucial to the courtroom issues
(55) that the witness's memories are supposed to resolve. For example, a perpetrator's shirt color or hairstyle might be tangential to one's shocked observance of an armed robbery, but later those factors might be crucial to establishing the identity of the perpetrator.

20. Which one of the following most accurately expresses the main point of the passage?

(A) The unreliability of memories about incidental aspects of observed events makes eyewitness testimony especially questionable in cases in which the witness was not directly involved.

(B) Because of the nature of human memory storage and retrieval, the courtroom testimony of eyewitnesses may contain crucial inaccuracies due to leading questions asked prior to the courtroom appearance.

(C) Researchers are surprised to find that courtroom testimony is often dependent on suggestion to fill gaps left by insufficient attention to detail at the time that the incident in question occurred.

(D) Although judges can disallow leading questions from the courtroom, it is virtually impossible to prevent them from being used elsewhere, to the detriment of many cases.

(E) Stricter regulation should be placed on lawyers whose leading questions can corrupt witnesses' testimony by introducing inaccurate data prior to the witnesses' appearance in the courtroom.

21. It can be reasonably inferred from the passage that which of the following, if it were effectively implemented, would most increase the justice system's ability to prevent leading questions from causing mistaken court decisions?

(A) a policy ensuring that witnesses have extra time to answer questions concerning details that are tangential to their original experiences of events

(B) thorough revision of the criteria for determining which kinds of interrogation may be disallowed in courtroom testimony under the category of "leading questions"

(C) increased attention to the nuances of all witnesses' responses to courtroom questions, even those that are not leading questions

(D) extensive interviewing of witnesses by all lawyers for both sides of a case prior to those witnesses' courtroom appearance

(E) availability of accurate transcripts of all interrogations of witnesses that occurred prior to those witnesses' appearance in court

22. Which one of the following is mentioned in the passage as a way in which new data suggested to a witness by a leading question are sometimes processed?

(A) They are integrated with current memories as support for those memories.

(B) They are stored tentatively as conjectural data that fade with time.

(C) They stay more vivid in memory than do previously stored memory data.

(D) They are reinterpreted so as to be compatible with the details already stored in memory.

(E) They are retained in memory even when they conflict with previously stored memory data.

23. In discussing the tangential details of events, the passage contrasts their original significance to witnesses with their possible significance in the courtroom (lines 52–59). That contrast is most closely analogous to which one of the following?

For purposes of flavor and preservation, salt and vinegar are important additions to cucumbers during the process of pickling, but these purposes could be attained by adding other ingredients instead.

(A)  For the purpose of adding a mild stimulant effect, caffeine is included in some types of carbonated drinks, but for the purposes of appealing to health-conscious consumers, some types of carbonated drinks are advertised as being caffeine-free.

(B)  For purposes of flavor and tenderness, the skins of apples and some other fruits are removed during preparation for drying, but grape skins are an essential part of raisins, and thus grape skins are not removed.

(C)  For purposes of flavor and appearance, wheat germ is not needed in flour and is usually removed during milling, but for purposes of nutrition, the germ is an important part of the grain.

(D)  For purposes of texture and appearance, some fat may be removed from meat when it is ground into sausage, but the removal of fat is also important for purposes of health.

24. Which one of the following questions is most directly answered by information in the passage?

(A)  In witnessing what types of crimes are people especially likely to pay close attention to circumstantial details?

(B)  Which aspects of courtroom interrogation cause witnesses to be especially reluctant to testify in extensive detail?

(C)  Can the stress of having to testify in a courtroom situation affect the accuracy of memory storage and retrieval?

(D)  Do different people tend to possess different capacities for remembering details correctly?

(E)  When is it more likely that a detail of an observed event will be accurately remembered?

25. The second paragraph consists primarily of material that

(A)  corroborates and adds detail to a claim made in the first paragraph

(B)  provides examples illustrating the applications of a theory discussed in the first paragraph

(C)  forms an argument in support of a proposal that is made in the final paragraph

(D)  anticipates and provides grounds for the rejection of a theory alluded to by the author in the final paragraph

(E)  explains how newly obtained data favor one of two traditional theories mentioned elsewhere in the second paragraph

26. It can be most reasonably inferred from the passage that the author holds that the recent studies discussed in the passage

(A)  have produced some unexpected findings regarding the extent of human reliance on external verification of memory details

(B)  shed new light on a longstanding procedural controversy in the law

(C)  may be of theoretical interest despite their tentative nature and inconclusive findings

(D)  provide insights into the origins of several disparate types of logically fallacious reasoning

(E)  should be of more than abstract academic interest to the legal profession

27. Which one of the following can be most reasonably inferred from the information in the passage?

(A)  The tendency of leading questions to cause unreliable courtroom testimony has no correlation with the extent to which witnesses are emotionally affected by the events that they have observed.

(B)  Leading questions asked in the process of a courtroom examination of a witness are more likely to cause inaccurate testimony than are leading questions asked outside the courtroom.

(C)  The memory processes by which newly introduced data tend to reinforce accurately remembered details of events are not relevant to explaining the effects of leading questions.

(D)  The risk of testimony being inaccurate due to certain other factors tends to increase as an eyewitness's susceptibility to giving inaccurate testimony due to the effects of leading questions increases.

(E)  The traditional grounds on which leading questions can be excluded from courtroom interrogation of witnesses have been called into question by the findings of recent studies.

# SOLUTIONS: The 180 Experience

The following is a real-time solution given from the perspective of a 180-level test-taker. Later on, we'll present a more detailed and thorough analysis. For now, notice how the lessons presented earlier in this book come together under "actual conditions." This test-taker has internalized the approaches, and has reached the point where he can make quick decisions based on hours of practice, review, and analysis.

> Background information on multipolar international systems

Social scientists have traditionally defined multipolar international systems as consisting of three or more nations, each of roughly equal military and economic strength. Theoretically, the members of such
(5) systems create shifting, temporary alliances in response to changing circumstances in the international environment. Such systems are, thus, fluid and flexible. Frequent, small confrontations are one attribute of multipolar systems and are usually the result of less
(10) powerful members grouping together to counter threats from larger, more aggressive members seeking hegemony. Yet the constant and inevitable counterbalancing typical of such systems usually results in stability. The best-known example of a
(15) multipolar system is the Concert of Europe, which coincided with general peace on that continent lasting roughly 100 years beginning around 1815.

> Multipolar systems stable.

> Background information on bipolar systems. Comparison between multi- and bipolar.

Bipolar systems, on the other hand, involve two major members of roughly equal military and
(20) economic strength vying for power and advantage. Other members of lesser strength tend to coalesce around one or the other pole. Such systems tend to be rigid and fixed, in part due to the existence of only one axis of power. Zero-sum political and military
(25) maneuverings, in which a gain for one side results in an equivalent loss for the other, are a salient feature of bipolar systems. Overall superiority is sought by both major members which can lead to frequent confrontations, debilitating armed conflict, and,
(30) eventually, to the capitulation of one or the other side. Athens and Sparta of ancient Greece had a bipolar relationship, as did the United States and the USSR during the Cold War.

> Bipolar systems unstable. The comparison is complete, but we don't have an argument yet.

> Here comes the argument.

However, the shift in the geopolitical landscape
(35) following the end of the Cold War calls for a reassessment of the assumptions underlying these two theoretical concepts. The emerging but still vague multipolar system in Europe today brings with it the unsettling prospect of new conflicts and shifting
(40) alliances that may lead to a diminution, rather than an enhancement, of security. The frequent, small confrontations that are thought to have kept the

> Now multipolar systems are unstable.

8

Concert of Europe in a state of equilibrium would today, as nations arm themselves with modern
(45) weapons, create instability that could destroy the system. And the larger number of members and shifting alliance patterns peculiar to multipolar systems would create a bewildering tangle of conflicts.

This reassessment may also lead us to look at the
(50) Cold War in a new light. In 1914 smaller members of the multipolar system in Europe brought the larger members into a war that engulfed the continent. The aftermath—a crippled system in which certain members were dismantled, punished, or voluntarily
(55) withdrew—created the conditions that led to World War II. In contrast, the principal attributes of bipolar systems—two major members with only one possible axis of conflict locked in a rigid yet usually stable struggle for power—may have created the necessary
(60) parameters for general peace in the second half of the twentieth century.

> And this bipolar system that brought cold war also brought general peace/ stability.

1. Which one of the following most accurately expresses the main point of the passage?

(A̶) Peace can be maintained in Europe only if a new bipolar system emerges to replace Cold War alliances.

(B̶) All kinds of international systems discussed by social scientists carry within themselves the seeds of their own collapse and ultimately endanger international order.

(C̶) The current European geopolitical landscape is a multipolar system that strongly resembles the Concert of Europe which existed through most of the nineteenth century.

(D) Multipolarity fostered the conditions that led to World War II and is incompatible with a stable, modern Europe.

(E) The characterization of multipolar systems as stable and bipolar systems as open to debilitating conflict needs to be reconsidered in light of the realities of post-Cold War Europe.

> Can quickly eliminate (A), (B), and (C).

> (D) seems too strong. Passage is not that absolute.
>
> (E) matches reading process.
>
> (E) is correct.

8

Before looking at answers, looked back at final paragraph. Remembered that its purpose was to support argument that in modern world, multi- might be unstable and bi- might be stable.

Can quickly eliminate (A), (B), and (E).

2. Which one of the following statements most accurately describes the function of the final paragraph?

(A) The weaknesses of both types of systems are discussed in the context of twentieth-century European history.

(B) A prediction is made regarding European security based on the attributes of both types of systems.

(C) A new argument is introduced in favor of European countries embracing a new bipolar system.

(D) Twentieth-century European history is used to expand on the argument in the previous paragraph.

(E) The typical characteristics of the major members of a bipolar system are reviewed.

(C) seems too strong. The author makes no direct mention of Europe embracing a new system.

(D) makes sense. In the previous paragraph, author introduced his or her side of an argument, and final paragraph supports that side.

(D) is correct.

**8**

Before looking at answers, reread those lines and the ones immediately before and after. Remembered that the purpose of that paragraph was to show that bipolar systems are historically unstable.

Can quickly eliminate (B), (D), (E).

3. The author's reference to the possibility that confrontations may lead to capitulation (lines 27–30) serves primarily to

(A) indicate that bipolar systems can have certain unstable characteristics

(B) illustrate how multipolar systems can transform themselves into bipolar systems

(C) contrast the aggressive nature of bipolar members with the more rational behavior of their multipolar counterparts

(D) indicate the anarchic nature of international relations

(E) suggest that military and economic strength shifts in bipolar as frequently as in multipolar systems

This is a hard question.

(A) seems like exactly the answer I am looking for, but...

(C) seems like it's correct too. Seems to say something very similar to (A). I read (C) more carefully. Did the passage say bipolar are aggressive and multipolar *rational*? No. It's a similar idea to (A), but it's not supported.

(A) is the correct answer.

Before looking at answers, remembered that the Cold War is mostly mentioned in the final paragraph, which I already understand the role of.

Can quickly eliminate (A), (B), (D), and (E).

4. With respect to the Cold War, the author's attitude can most accurately be described as

(A) fearful that European geopolitics may bring about a similar bipolar system

(B) surprised that it did not end with a major war

(C) convinced that it provides an important example of bipolarity maintaining peace

(D) regretful that the major European countries were so ambivalent about it

(E) confident it will mark only a brief hiatus between long periods of European multipolarity

(C) is the only viable answer, and it matches my understanding of the argument.

(C) is the correct answer.

Before looking at answers, reread those lines. Purpose of them in argument is evidence for idea that multipolar systems tend to bring peace.

Can quickly eliminate (A), (C), and (E).

5. Which one of the following statements concerning the concert of Europe (lines 14–17) can most reasonably be inferred from the passage?

(A) Each of the many small confrontations that occurred under the Concert of Europe threatened the integrity of the system.

(B) It provided the highest level of security possible for Europe in the late nineteenth century.

(C) All the factors contributing to stability during the late nineteenth century continue to contribute to European security.

(D) Equilibrium in the system was maintained as members grouped together to counterbalance mutual threats.

(E) It was more stable than most multipolar systems because its smaller members reacted promptly to aggression by its larger members.

Total time: 4:50
Reading: 2:15
Questions: 2:35

(B) seems too extreme. I've only been told about two systems, so I can't really say it provides the highest level of security possible.

(D) doesn't seem right at first, but I go back to the text and see that this very idea was discussed just a few lines before, and the concert of Europe is in support of that idea.

(D) is the correct answer.

8

**Starts with (main) opinion. L.A. poetry differs from Spanish poetry.**

**Hint of possible other side of argument—unity between L.A. and Spanish poetry.**

**Author quickly refutes.**

**One example of how they are different.**

**Another example of how they are different.**

**Another example of how they are different.**

**Twist: modern poetry, but also pulling inspiration from imagining a way distant past.**

8

In spite of a shared language, Latin American poetry written in Spanish differs from Spanish poetry in many respects. The Spanish of Latin American poets is more open than that of Spanish poets, more exposed
(5) to outside influences—indigenous, English, French, and other languages. While some literary critics maintain that there is as much linguistic unity in Latin American poetry as there is in Spanish poetry, they base this claim on the fact that Castilian Spanish, the
(10) official and literary version of the Spanish language based largely on the dialect originally spoken in the Castile region of Spain, was transplanted to the Americas when it was already a relatively standardized idiom. Although such unity may have characterized the
(15) earliest Latin American poetry, after centuries in the Americas the language of Lain American poetry cannot help but reveal the influences of its unique cultural history.

Latin American poetry is critical or irreverent in its
(20) attitude toward language, where that of Spanish poets is more accepting. For example, the Spanish-language incarnations of modernism and the avant-garde, two literary movements that used language in innovative and challenging ways, originated with Latin American
(25) poets. By contrast, when these movements later reached Spain, Spanish poets greeted them with reluctance. Spanish poets, even those of the modern era, seem to take their language for granted, rarely using it in radical or experimental ways.

(30) The most distinctive note in Latin American poetry is its enthusiastic response to the modern world, while Spanish poetry displays a kind of cultural conservatism—the desire to return to an ideal culture of the distant past. Because no Spanish-language
(35) culture lies in the equally distant (i.e., pre-Columbian) past of the Americas, but has instead been invented by Latin Americans day by day, Latin American poetry has no such long-standing past to romanticize. Instead, Latin American poetry often displays a curiosity about
(40) the literature of other cultures, an interest in exploring poetic structures beyond those typical of Spanish poetry. For example, the first Spanish-language haiku—a Japanese poetic form—were written by José Juan Tablada, a Mexican. Another of the Latin
(45) American poets' responses to this absence is the search for a world before recorded history—not only that of Spain or the Americas, but in some cases of the planet; the Chilean poet Pablo Neruda's work, for example, is noteworthy for its development of an ahistorical
(50) mythology for the creation of the earth. For Latin American poets there is no such thing as the pristine cultural past affirmed in the poetry of Spain: there is only the fluid interaction of all world cultures, or else the extensive time before cultures began.

6. The discussion in the second paragraph is intended primarily to

(A) argue that Latin American poets originated modernism and the avant-garde

(B) explain how Spanish poetry and Latin American poetry differ in their attitudes toward the Spanish language

(C) demonstrate why Latin American poetry is not well received in Spain

(D) show that the Castilian Spanish employed in Spanish poetry has remained relatively unchanged by the advent of modernism and the avant-garde

(E) illustrate the extent to which Spanish poetry romanticizes Spanish-language culture.

> Before looking at answers, recall second paragraph meant to show differences in how Latin American and Spanish poets view language.
>
> Can quickly eliminate (A), (C), (D), and (E).

> (B) is only remaining choice and it matches my thought process.
>
> (B) is the correct answer.

7. Given the information in the passage, which one of the following is most analogous to the evolution of Latin American poetry?

(A) A family moves its restaurant to a new town and incorporates local ingredients into its traditional recipes.

(B) A family moves its business to a new town after the business fails in its original location.

(C) A family with a two-hundred-year-old house labors industriously in order to restore the house to its original appearance.

(D) A family does research into its ancestry in order to construct its family tree.

(E) A family eagerly anticipates its annual vacation but never takes photographs or purchases souvenirs to preserve its memories.

> Very general prompt. Nothing to look at beforehand.
>
> Can quickly eliminate (B), (C), (D), and (E).

> (A) seemed to match, and none of the other choices make sense.
>
> (A) is the correct answer.

8

**Very general prompt. Nothing to look at beforehand.**

**Can quickly eliminate (D) and (E).**

8. The passage's claims about Spanish poetry would be most weakened if new evidence indicating which one of the following were discovered?

(A) Spanish linguistic constructs had greater influence on Latin American poets than had previously been thought.

(B) Castilian Spanish was still evolving linguistically at the time of the inception of Latin American poetry.

(C) Spanish poets originated an influential literary movement that used language in radical ways.

(D̸) Castilian Spanish was influenced during its evolution by other Spanish dialects.

(E̸) Spanish poets rejected the English and French incarnations of modernism.

**(A) and (B) seemed like potential answers until I got to (C). (C) represents exactly the opposite of the author's main point about Spanish poetry: that it did NOT use language in radical ways.**

**(C) is the correct answer.**

**Can quickly eliminate (A), (B), (C), and (E) because I remember seeing each of these in the passage.**

9. The passage affirms each of the following EXCEPT:

(A̸) The first haiku in the Spanish language were written by a Latin American poet.

(B̸) Spanish poetry is rarely innovative or experimental in its use of language.

(C̸) Spanish poetry rarely incorporates poetic traditions from other cultures.

(D) Latin American poetry tends to take the Spanish language for granted.

(E̸) Latin American poetry incorporates aspects of various other languages.

**(D) is the obvious choice here. The author never says anything negative about the Latin American writers, certainly not that they take the Spanish language for granted. In fact, it says Spanish poets took language for granted.**

**(D) is the correct answer.**

**8**

10. Which one of the following can most reasonably
    be inferred from the passage about Latin
    American poetry's use of poetic structures from
    other world cultures?

Can quickly eliminate
(A), (C), (D), and (E).

(A) The use of poetic structures from other world
    cultures is an attempt by Latin American poets to
    create a cultural past.

(B) The use of poetic structures from other world
    cultures by Latin American poets is a response to
    their lack of a long-standing Spanish-language
    cultural past in the Americas.

(C) The use of poetic structures from other world
    cultures has led Latin American poets to
    reconsider their lack of a long-standing Spanish-
    language cultural past in the Americas.

(D) Latin American poets who write about a world
    before recorded history do not use poetic
    structures from other world cultures.

(E) Latin American poetry does not borrow poetic
    structures from other world cultures whose
    literature exhibits cultural conservatism.

(B) seems like the only
viable answer. Checked
against text. Found proof in
final paragraph.

(B) is the correct answer.

11. Based on the passage, the author most likely holds
    which one of the following views toward Spanish
    poetry's relationship to the Spanish cultural past?

Before looking at
answers, reread
beginning of final
paragraph, which
describes Spanish
poets' relationship to
Spanish history.

Can quickly eliminate
(B) and (E).

(A) This relationship has inspired Spanish poets to
    examine their cultural past with a critical eye.

(B) This relationship forces Spanish poets to write
    about subjects with which they feel little natural
    affinity.

(C) This relationship is itself the central theme of
    much Spanish poetry.

(D) This relationship infuses Spanish poetry with a
    romanticism that is reluctant to embrace the
    modern era.

(E) This relationship results in poems that are of little
    interest to contemporary Spanish readers.

"Critical" in (A) is the
wrong word.

(C) seems attractive,
but wasn't specifically
mentioned in text.

(D) matches up with
the text. We know
the Spanish were
reluctant to embrace
modernity.

(D) is the correct
answer.

8

This is hard. No obvious wrongs here. Have to concentrate on specific details.

12. Which one of the following inferences is most supported by the passage?

(A) A tradition of cultural conservatism has allowed the Spanish language to evolve into a stable, reliable form of expression.

(B) It was only recently that Latin American poetry began to incorporate elements of other languages.

(C) The cultural conservatism of Spanish poetry is exemplified by the uncritical attitude of Spanish poets toward the Spanish language.

(D) Latin American poets' interest in other world cultures is illustrated by their use of Japanese words and phrases.

(E) Spanish poetry is receptive to the influence of some Spanish-language poets outside of Spain.

(A) seems attractive, but there is no evidence that backs up connection between cultural conservatism and a stable Spanish language.

(B) depends on your definition of "recent" but doesn't match up with text, which seems to indicate that LA poetry started incorporating early.

(C) can possibly be inferred because they say LA poets looked at language critically, and Spanish were more accepting. But pretty weak.

(D) is incorrect in the details. They were inspired by Japanese form, but not actual Japanese words and phrases.

(E) seems like a "trick" right answer, because "some" is a relatively easy thing to prove. However, there is nothing in the text that allows me to make this logic leap.

(C) is the best available answer.

**Total time: 7:10**
**Reading: 3:50**
**Questions: 3:20**

Note: The passage was very hard to get through and understand, but the questions ended up being pretty straightforward overall.

Background information. The general subject area is gravity.

According the the theory of gravitation, every particle of matter in the universe attracts every other particle with a force that increases as either the mass of the particle increase, or their proximity to one
(5) another increases, or both. Gravitation is believed to shape the structures of stars, galaxies, and the entire universe. But for decades cosmologists (scientists who study the universe) have attempted to account for the finding that at least 90 percent of the universe seems to
(10) be missing: that the total amount of observable matter—stars,dust, and miscellaneous debris—does not contain enough mass to explain why the universe is organized in the shape of galaxies and clusters of galaxies. To account for this discrepancy, cosmologists
(15) hypothesize that something else, which they call "dark matter," provides the gravitational force necessary to make the huge structures cohere.

This is the mystery that the passage will try to solve.

This is one side of the argument (call it side A): dark matter solves gravitational mystery.

What is dark matter? Numerous exotic entities have been postulated, but among the more attractive
(20) candidates—because they are known actually to exist—are neutrinos, elementary particles created as a by-product of nuclear fusion, radioactive decay, or catastrophic collisions between other particles. Neutrinos, which come in three types, are by far the
(25) most numerous kind of particle in the universe; however, they have long been assumed to have no mass. If so, that would disqualify them as dark matter. Without mass, matter cannot exert gravitational force; without such force, it cannot induce other matter to
(30) cohere.

Evidence for the other side: dark matter doesn't solve mystery (call it side B).

Refutes side B, support for side A of argument.

But new evidence suggests that a neutrino does have mass. This evidence came by way of research findings supporting the existence of a long-theorized but never observed phenomenon called oscillation,
(35) whereby each of the three neutrino types can change into one of the others as it travels through space. Researchers held that the transformation is possible only if neutrinos also have mass. They obtained experimental confirmation of the theory by generating
(40) one neutrino type and then finding evidence that it had oscillated into the predicted neutrino type. In the process, they were able to estimate the mass of a neutrino at from 0.5 to 5 electron volts.

8

While slight, even the lowest estimate would yield
(45) a lot of mass given that neutrinos are so numerous, especially considering that neutrinos were previously assumed to have no mass. Still, even at the highest estimate, neutrinos could only account for about 20 percent of the universe's "missing" mass.

Evidence for the other side, side B.

Support for side A, but softening of argument. Dark matter isn't a complete explanation, but it offers promise.

(50) Nevertheless, that is enough to alter our picture of the universe even if it does not account for all of dark matter. In fact, some cosmologists claim that this new evidence offers the best theoretical solution yet to the dark matter problem. If the evidence holds up, these
(55) cosmologists believe, it may add to our understanding of the role elementary particles play in holding the universe together.

13. Which one of the following most accurately expresses the main idea of the passage?

(A) Although cosmologists believe that the universe is shaped by gravitation, the total amount of observable matter in the universe is greatly insufficient to account for the gravitation that would be required to cause the universe to be organized into galaxies.

(B) Given their inability to account for more than 20 percent of the universe's "missing" mass, scientists are beginning to speculate that our current understanding of gravity is significantly mistaken.

(C) Indirect evidence suggesting that neutrinos have mass may allow neutrinos to account for up to 20 percent of dark matter, a finding that could someday be extended to a complete solution of the dark matter problem.

(D) After much speculation, researchers have discovered that neutrinos oscillate from one type into another as they travel through space, a phenomenon that proves that neutrinos have mass.

(E) Although it has been established that neutrinos have mass, such mass does not support the speculation of cosmologists that neutrinos constitute a portion of the universe's "missing" mass.

> Before looking at answers, remind myself of general argument (dark matter is solution to gravity mystery), and structure relative to argument.
>
> Can quickly eliminate (A), (B), (D), and (E).
>
> (A), (B), and (E) misrepresent the author's opinion, and (D) is too narrow in scope.

> (C) is not a great summary, but it is the best available.
>
> (C) is the correct answer.

14. Which one of the following titles most completely and accurately expresses the contents of the passage?

(A) "The Existence of Dark Matter: Arguments For and Against"

(B) "Neutrinos and the Dark Matter Problem: A Partial Solution?"

(C) "Too Little, Too Late: Why Neutrinos Do Not Constitute Dark Matter"

(D) "The Role of Gravity: How Dark Matter Shapes Stars"

(E) "The Implications of Oscillation: Do Neutrinos Really Have Mass?"

> Can quickly eliminate (C) and (E).
>
> (C) misrepresents the author's opinion, and (E) is too narrow in scope.

> After I eliminate (C) and (E), I eliminate (A). There isn't a lot of evidence given that goes *against* the idea that dark matter exists. (B) and (D) are both attractive, but the passage doesn't actually discuss *how* dark matter shapes stars.
>
> (B) is the correct answer.

**8**

15. Based on the passage, the author most likely holds which one of the following views?

Open-ended prompt.

Can quickly eliminate (A), (C), and (E).

(A̶) Observable matter constitutes at least 90 percent of the mass of the universe.

(B) Current theories are incapable of identifying the force that causes all particles in the universe to attract one another.

(C̶) The key to the problem of dark matter is determining the exact mass of a neutrino.

(D) is unlikely that any force other than gravitation will be required to account for the organization of the universe into galaxies.

(E̶) probably account for most of the universe's "missing" mass.

I don't think (B) is correct. Isn't that force gravity?

(D) makes sense. The author seems to believe that, though the current explanation for dark matter and gravity is incomplete, it is on the right track.

(D) is the correct answer.

16. As described in the last paragraph of the passage, the cosmologists' approach to solving the dark matter problem is most analogous to which one of the following?

Before reading answers, reread last paragraph.

Cosmologists believe that, even though explanation is incomplete, it is on the right track.

Can quickly eliminate (B), (C), and (E).

(A) A child seeking information about how to play chess consults a family member and so learns of a book that will instruct her in the game.

(B̶) A child seeking to earn money by delivering papers is unable to earn enough money for a bicycle and so decides to buy a skateboard instead.

(C̶) A child hoping to get a dog for his birthday is initially disappointed when his parents bring home a cat but eventually learns to love the animal.

(D) A child seeking money to attend a movie is given some of the money by one of his siblings and so decides to go to each of his other siblings to ask for additional money.

(E̶) A child enjoys playing sports with the neighborhood children but her parents insist that she cannot participate until she has completed her household chores.

(A) seems close, but I'm not sure what the family member and book are analogous to in the passage. Furthermore, the instruction book is a step removed from the chess, but neutrinos are not a step removed from dark matter—they *are* dark matter.

(D) seems to match better. Neutrinos may account for some of the missing mass; now the cosmologists will seek the rest.

Tough question, but (D) is better than (A).

(D) is the correct answer.

8

Before reading answers, reread the part on oscillation. The author doesn't seem to have an attitude about it. Seems like he is giving objective information.

Can quickly eliminate (B), (C), (D), and (E).

17. The author's attitude towards oscillation can most accurately be characterized as being

(A) satisfied that it occurs and that it suggests that neutrinos have mass

(B̸) hopeful that it will be useful in discovering other forms of dark matter

(C̸) concerned that it is often misinterpreted to mean that neutrinos account for all of dark matter

(D̸) skeptical that it occurs until further research can be done

(E̸) convinced that it cannot occur outside an experimental setting

(A) seems true, and the other answers have obvious flaws.

(A) is the correct answer.

Before looking at answers, reread from a couple of lines before. To me, cohere in this case means "bring things together" (that's what gravitational force does).

Can quickly eliminate (C), (D), and (E).

18. Which one of the following phrases could replace the world "cohere" at line 29 without substantively altering the author's meaning?

(A) exert gravitational force

(B) form galactic structures

(C̸) oscillate into another type of matter

(D̸) become significantly more massive

(E̸) fuse to produce new particles

Exert gravitational force isn't right—the sentence wouldn't make sense. I didn't think initially of "form galactic structures," but I guess that is what gravity does when it brings things together.

(B) is the correct answer.

19. The passage states each of the following EXCEPT:

**8**

I don't remember seeing (A), but I remember and can quickly eliminate (B), (D), and (E).

(A) There are more neutrinos in the universe than there are non-neutrinos.

(B̸) Observable matter cannot exert enough gravitational force to account for the present structure of the universe.

(C) Scientific experiments support the theory of neutrino oscillation.

(D̸) Neutrinos likely cannot account for all of the universe's "missing" mass.

(E̸) Dark matter may account for a large portion of the universe's gravitational force.

Double-checked (C) against text. It's in there.

(A) is the correct answer.

Total time: 8:20
Reading: 3:30
Questions: 4:50

Leading questions—questions worded in such a way as to suggest a particular answer—can yield unreliable testimony either by design, as when a lawyer tries to trick a witness into affirming a particular
(5)   version of the evidence of a case, or by accident, when a questioner unintentionally prejudices the witness's response. For this reason, a judge can disallow such questions in the courtroom interrogation of witnesses. But their exclusion from the courtroom by no means
(10)  eliminates the remote effects of earlier leading questions on eyewitness testimony. Alarmingly, the beliefs about an event that a witness brings to the courtroom may often be adulterated by the effects of leading questions that were introduced intentionally or
(15)  unintentionally by lawyers, police investigators, reporters, or others with whom the witness has already interacted.

Recent studies have confirmed the ability of leading questions to alter the details of our memories
(20)  and have led to a better understanding of how this process occurs and, perhaps, of the conditions that make for greater risks that an eyewitness's memories have been tainted by leading questions. These studies suggest that not all details of our experiences become
(25)  clearly or stably stored in memory—only those to which we give adequate attention. Moreover, experimental evidence indicates that if subtly introduced new data involving remembered events do not actively conflict with our stored memory data, we
(30)  tend to process such new data similarly whether they correspond to details as we remember them, or to gaps in those details. In the former case, we often retain the new data as a reinforcement of the corresponding aspect of the memory, and in the latter case, we often
(35)  retain them as a construction to fill the corresponding gap. An eyewitness who is asked, prior to courtroom testimony, "How fast was the car going when it passed the stop sign?" may respond to the query about speed without addressing the question of the stop sign. But
(40)  the "stop sign" datum has now been introduced, and when later recalled, perhaps during courtroom testimony, it may be processed as belonging to the original memory even if the witness actually saw no stop sign.
(45)  The farther removed from the event, the greater the chance of a vague or incomplete recollection and the greater the likelihood of newly suggested information blending with original memories. Since we can be more easily misled with respect to fainter and more
(50)  uncertain memories, tangential details are more apt to become constructed out of subsequently introduced information than are more central details. But what is tangential to a witness's original experience of an event may nevertheless be crucial to the courtroom issues
(55)  that the witness's memories are supposed to resolve.

Background information about danger of leading questions, and why judges can disallow them.

This is likely one side of a mostly one-sided argument: A witness's beliefs about an incident can be adulterated in many ways.

Support for the argument.

More support for the argument.

8

For example, a perpetrator's shirt color or hairstyle might be tangential to one's shocked observance of an armed robbery, but later those factors might be crucial to establishing the identity of the perpetrator.

Seemed like a pretty straightforward, objective passage about different ways our memories of events can be altered, and how this relates in particular to witnesses.

Can quickly eliminate (C).

20. Which one of the following most accurately expresses the main point of the passage?

(A) The unreliability of memories about incidental aspects of observed events makes eyewitness testimony especially questionable in cases in which the witness was not directly involved.

(B) Because of the nature of human memory storage and retrieval, the courtroom testimony of eyewitnesses may contain crucial inaccuracies due to leading questions asked prior to the courtroom appearance.

(C̸) Researchers are surprised to find that courtroom testimony is often dependent on suggestion to fill gaps left by insufficient attention to detail at the time that the incident in question occurred.

(D) Although judges can disallow leading questions from the courtroom, it is virtually impossible to prevent them from being used elsewhere, to the detriment of many cases.

(E) Stricter regulation should be placed on lawyers whose leading questions can corrupt witnesses' testimony by introducing inaccurate data prior to the witnesses' appearance in the courtroom.

The rest of the choices seem pretty attractive. I reexamine them one at a time, suspicious of all details.

(A) is wrong—it didn't discuss whether or not the witness is directly involved.

(B) doesn't seem like a great answer, but it doesn't have obvious flaws.

(D) is wrong. That's not the main point of the passage.

(E) presumes too much. The author didn't say anything about regulations, etc.

(B) is the correct answer.

8

21. It can be reasonably inferred from the passage that which of the following, if it were effectively implemented, would most increase the justice system's ability to prevent leading questions from causing mistaken court decisions?

Can quickly eliminate (A), (C), and (D).

(A̸) a policy ensuring that witnesses have extra time to answer questions concerning details that are tangential to their original experiences of events

(B) thorough revision of the criteria for determining which kinds of interrogation may be disallowed in courtroom testimony under the category of "leading questions"

(C̸) increased attention to the nuances of all witnesses' responses to courtroom questions, even those that are not leading questions

(D̸) extensive interviewing of witnesses by all lawyers for both sides of a case prior to those witnesses' courtroom appearance

(E) availability of accurate transcripts of all interrogations of witnesses that occurred prior to those witnesses' appearance in court

(B) is attractive, but the passage is in large part about stuff that happens before the courtroom testimony.

If I have transcripts, I might be able to see how leading questions might have shaped a witness's memory.

(E) is the correct answer.

22. Which one of the following is mentioned in the passage as a way in which new data suggested to a witness by a leading question are sometimes processed?

Can quickly eliminate (B), (C), and (E).

(A) They are integrated with current memories as support for those memories.

(B̸) They are stored tentatively as conjectural data that fade with time.

(C̸) They stay more vivid in memory than do previously stored memory data.

(D) They are reinterpreted so as to be compatible with the details already stored in memory.

(E̸) They are retained in memory even when they conflict with previously stored memory data.

(A) and (D) both sound attractive. I go back and reread the relevant text (32–36).

Seems to support (A).

(D) can't be right because there has been nothing about *reinterpreting* new data.

(A) is the correct answer.

**8**

23. In discussing the tangential details of events, the passage contrasts their original significance to witnesses with their possible significance in the courtroom (lines 52–59). That contrast is most closely analogous to which one of the following?

> More support for the argument.

(A̶) For purposes of flavor and preservation, salt and vinegar are important additions to cucumbers during the process of pickling, but these purposes could be attained by adding other ingredients instead.

(B̶) For the purpose of adding a mild stimulant effect, caffeine is included in some types of carbonated drinks, but for the purposes of appealing to health-conscious consumers, some types of carbonated drinks are advertised as being caffeine-free.

> Both (D) and (E) contain elements that are unimportant for one consideration and important for another. In (D), two contrasting elements, but in (E), two positive elements. Our original situation is a contrasting one.
>
> (D) is the correct answer.

(C̶) For purposes of flavor and tenderness, the skins of apples and some other fruits are removed during preparation for drying, but grape skins are an essential part of raisins, and thus grape skins are not removed.

(D) For purposes of flavor and appearance, wheat germ is not needed in flour and is usually removed during milling, but for purposes of nutrition, the germ is an important part of the grain.

(E) For purposes of texture and appearance, some fat may be removed from meat when it is ground into sausage, but the removal of fat is also important for purposes of health.

> Before reading the answers, reread final paragraph. Quick self-summary: we are more likely to switch around elements that we pay less critical attention to, and these elements may play a critical role in a case.
>
> Can quickly eliminate (A), (B), and (C).

24. Which one of the following questions is most directly answered by information in the passage?

(A) In witnessing what types of crimes are people especially likely to pay close attention to circumstantial details?

(B̶) Which aspects of courtroom interrogation cause witnesses to be especially reluctant to testify in extensive detail?

(C̶) Can the stress of having to testify in a courtroom situation affect the accuracy of memory storage and retrieval?

(D̶) Do different people tend to possess different capacities for remembering details correctly?

(E) When is it more likely that a detail of an observed event will be accurately remembered?

> Can quickly eliminate (B), (C), and (D).

> (A) sounded attractive at first, but "types of crimes" isn't mentioned.
>
> (E) makes sense. Several parts of the passage mention scenarios (not being far removed from event, not being asked about tangential details) that make it more likely a person will accurately remember a detail.
>
> (E) is the correct answer.

MANHATTAN
LSAT

25. The second paragraph consists primarily of material that

(A) corroborates and adds detail to a claim made in the first paragraph

(B) provides examples illustrating the applications of a theory discussed in the first paragraph

(C̶) forms an argument in support of a proposal that is made in the final paragraph

(D̶) anticipates and provides grounds for the rejection of a theory alluded to by the author in the final paragraph

(E̶) explains how newly obtained data favor one of two traditional theories mentioned elsewhere in the second paragraph

Before reading the answers, I return to the 2nd paragraph. I know the general purpose was to support the main opinion that came at the end of paragraph 1.

Can quickly eliminate (C), (D), and (E).

The argument is more of a claim than a theory. And they are not technically "applications."

(A) is the correct answer.

26. It can be most reasonably inferred from the passage that the author holds that the recent studies discussed in the passage

(A) have produced some unexpected findings regarding the extent of human reliance on external verification of memory details

(B̶) shed new light on a longstanding procedural controversy in the law

(C̶) may be of theoretical interest despite their tentative nature and inconclusive findings

(D̶) provide insights into the origins of several disparate types of logically fallacious reasoning

(E) should be of more than abstract academic interest to the legal profession

Can quickly eliminate (B), (C), and (D).

(A) is tempting because the author uses the word "alarmingly" in paragraph 1, but I don't think the author found the results unexpected.

(E) isn't directly mentioned, but you get the sense the author thinks this is a serious issue, and therefore one that deserves real-life (as opposed to purely academic) consideration.

(E) is the correct answer.

8

27. Which one of the following can be most reasonably inferred from the information in the passage?

(A) The tendency of leading questions to cause unreliable courtroom testimony has no correlation with the extent to which witnesses are emotionally affected by the events that they have observed.

(B) Leading questions asked in the process of a courtroom examination of a witness are more likely to cause inaccurate testimony than are leading questions asked outside the courtroom.

(C) The memory processes by which newly introduced data tend to reinforce accurately remembered details of events are not relevant to explaining the effects of leading questions.

(D) The risk of testimony being inaccurate due to certain other factors tends to increase as an eyewitness's susceptibility to giving inaccurate testimony due to the effects of leading questions increases.

(E) The traditional grounds on which leading questions can be excluded from courtroom interrogation of witnesses have been called into question by the findings of recent studies.

---

Can quickly eliminate (A), (B), (C), and (E).

---

(D) sounds really complicated, but it essentially means that risk of inaccuracy is greater when witness's susceptibility to giving inaccurate testimony because of leading questions is greater. That's exactly what a lot of the text is about.

(D) is the correct answer.

---

**Total time: 8:50**
**Reading: 2:50**
**Questions: 6:00**

8

# SOLUTIONS: Detailed Explanations

Social scientists have traditionally defined multipolar international systems as consisting of three or more nations, each of roughly equal military and economic strength. Theoretically, the members of such

(5) systems create shifting, temporary alliances in response to changing circumstances in the international environment. Such systems are, thus, fluid and flexible. Frequent, small confrontations are one attribute of multipolar systems and are usually the result of less

(10) powerful members grouping together to counter threats from larger, more aggressive members seeking hegemony. Yet the constant and inevitable counterbalancing typical of such systems usually results in stability. The best-known example of a

(15) multipolar system is the Concert of Europe, which coincided with general peace on that continent lasting roughly 100 years beginning around 1815.

Bipolar systems, on the other hand, involve two major members of roughly equal military and

(20) economic strength vying for power and advantage. Other members of lesser strength tend to coalesce around one or the other pole. Such systems tend to be rigid and fixed, in part due to the existence of only one axis of power. Zero-sum political and military

(25) maneuverings, in which a gain for one side results in an equivalent loss for the other, are a salient feature of bipolar systems. Overall superiority is sought by both major members which can lead to frequent confrontations, debilitating armed conflict, and,

(30) eventually, to the capitulation of one or the other side. Athens and Sparta of ancient Greece had a bipolar relationship, as did the United States and the USSR during the Cold War.

However, the shift in the geopolitical landscape

(35) following the end of the Cold War calls for a reassessment of the assumptions underlying these two theoretical concepts. The emerging but still vague multipolar system in Europe today brings with it the unsettling prospect of new conflicts and shifting

(40) alliances that may lead to a diminution, rather than an enhancement, of security. The frequent, small confrontations that are thought to have kept the Concert of Europe in a state of equilibrium would today, as nations arm themselves with modern

(45) weapons, create instability that could destroy the system. And the larger number of members and shifting alliance patterns peculiar to multipolar systems

would create a bewildering tangle of conflicts.

This reassessment may also lead us to look at the

(50) Cold War in a new light. In 1914 smaller members of the multipolar system in Europe brought the larger members into a war that engulfed the continent. The aftermath—a crippled system in which certain members were dismantled, punished, or voluntarily

(55) withdrew—created the conditions that led to World War II. In contrast, the principal attributes of bipolar systems—two major members with only one possible axis of conflict locked in a rigid yet usually stable struggle for power—may have created the necessary

(60) parameters for general peace in the second half of the twentieth century.

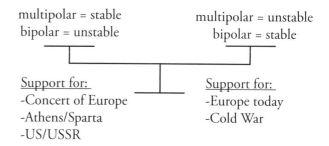

multipolar = stable                 multipolar = unstable
bipolar = unstable                  bipolar = stable

Support for:                        Support for:
-Concert of Europe                  -Europe today
-Athens/Sparta                      -Cold War
-US/USSR

*The passage discusses differences between multipolar systems and bipolar systems. It might seem that multipolar vs. bipolar will be the central argument, but this is merely a comparison, not an argument. The last two paragraphs discuss a reassessment of the traditional understanding of multipolar and bipolar systems. This reassessment is the central argument.*

*Note that the argument in this passage doesn't hinge on opinion (one group feels one way while another group feels another), but rather on situation; the author presents two different situations (historical vs. 20th century) that provide contrasting evidence relative to the characteristics of multipolar and bipolar systems.*

1. Which one of the following most accurately expresses the main point of the passage?

(A) Peace can be maintained in Europe only if a new bipolar system emerges to replace Cold War alliances.

(B) All kinds of international systems discussed by social scientists carry within themselves the seeds of their own collapse and ultimately endanger international order.

(C) The current European geopolitical landscape is a multipolar system that strongly resembles the Concert of Europe which existed through most of the nineteenth century.

(D) Multipolarity fostered the conditions that led to World War II and is incompatible with a stable, modern Europe.

(E) The characterization of multipolar systems as stable and bipolar systems as open to debilitating conflict needs to be reconsidered in light of the realities of post—Cold War Europe.

(A) **DEGREE (modifier).** Beware of words such as "only"; the author is not that absolute.
**SCOPE (out of scope).** Furthermore, this passage is not about how to maintain peace in the future.

(B) **DEGREE (modifier).** "All" is too strong.
**SCOPE (out of scope).** The author discusses only two kinds of international systems, not international systems in general. The scope of this answer is too broad.

(C) **INTERPRETATION (contradiction).** The passage states that the current European landscape is actually unstable whereas the Concert of Europe was stable.
**SCOPE (narrow).** Furthermore, this comparison is just one small part of the passage.

(D) **SCOPE (narrow).** This answer does not address the passage as a whole, but rather just one small part of it.
**DEGREE (opinion).** Furthermore, though the author is nervous about the multipolarity, "incompatible" is too strong a representation of the author's opinion.

(E) **CORRECT (synthesis).** This answer is a synthesis of various passage elements, and it matches our understanding of the scale.

2. Which one of the following statements most accurately describes the function of the final paragraph?

(A) The weaknesses of both types of systems are discussed in the context of twentieth-century European history.

(B) A prediction is made regarding European security based on the attributes of both types of systems.

(C) A new argument is introduced in favor of European countries embracing a new bipolar system.

(D) Twentieth-century European history is used to expand on the argument in the previous paragraph.

(E) The typical characteristics of the major members of a bipolar system are reviewed.

(A) **INTERPRETATION (unsupported).** Multipolar systems are described in terms of weaknesses, but bipolar systems are not.

(B) **SCOPE (out of scope).** A "prediction" is not made or discussed in any way.

(C) **DEGREE (opinion).** The author discusses the danger of multipolar systems and the stability brought on by bipolar systems, but does not go as far as to say that European countries should embrace a new system.

(D) **CORRECT (synthesis).** This answer correctly synthesizes information from the third and fourth paragraphs. In the third paragraph, the author says that, in the twentieth century, multipolar systems have been less stable and bipolar systems more stable. The examples in the final paragraph serve to support this argument.

(E) **INTERPRETATION (unsupported).** This is very subtle. The typical characteristics of bipolar systems are mentioned, but typical characteristics of the *major members* of a bipolar system are not discussed. Be careful how you interpret the details!

3. The author's reference to the possibility that confrontations may lead to capitulation (lines 27–30) serves primarily to

(A) indicate that bipolar systems can have certain unstable characteristics

(B) illustrate how multipolar systems can transform themselves into bipolar systems

(C) contrast the aggressive nature of bipolar members with the more rational behavior of their multipolar counterparts

(D) indicate the anarchic nature of international relations

(E) suggest that military and economic strength shifts in bipolar as frequently as in multipolar systems

(A) **CORRECT (inference).** These lines are used to support the idea that bipolar systems have traditionally been unstable.

(B) **INTERPRETATION (unsupported).** The author is comparing multipolar and bipolar systems, not discussing how one can become the other.

(C) **INTERPRETATION (unsupported).** This is a very attractive answer, but watch out for the details. Though bipolar systems seek superiority, it may not be because they are more aggressive by nature (perhaps they seek superiority because they think it will bring peace). Multipolar systems are described as being more stable historically, but not necessarily more rational.

(D) **SCOPE (out of scope).** This answer is too general. The passage is not about the anarchic nature of international relations.

(E) **INTERPRETATION (unsupported).** While the strength of nations within bipolar systems is discussed, nothing in the passage would support making a claim about the *frequency* of shifts in strength.

4. With respect to the Cold War, the author's attitude can most accurately be described as

(A) fearful that European geopolitics may bring about a similar bipolar system

(B) surprised that it did not end with a major war

(C) convinced that it provides an important example of bipolarity maintaining peace

(D) regretful that the major European countries were so ambivalent about it

(E) confident it will mark only a brief hiatus between long periods of European multipolarity

(A) **INTERPRETATION (unsupported).** There is no evidence to suggest that the author is fearful of bipolar systems.

(B) **INTERPRETATION (unsupported).** There is no evidence to suggest that the author is surprised.

(C) **CORRECT (inference).** This is a less than ideal answer, but correct nonetheless. Lines 56–60 state: "...the principal attributes of bipolar systems... *may have* created the necessary parameters for peace..." We are asked to infer from this statement that the author is "*convinced* that it provides an important example of bipolarity maintaining peace." "Convinced" is a very strong word given the context. While this isn't an ideal answer, it is certainly the best available.

(D) **SCOPE (out of scope).** European opinion about the Cold War is not a topic relevant to this discussion in any way.

(E) **INTERPRETATION (unsupported).** This answer strays too far from the text, and makes a leap in terms of how the author feels about the particular subject—how recent history relates to other history (e.g., this is a hiatus, or this represents a permanent change).

8

5. Which one of the following statements concerning the Concert of Europe (lines 14–17) can most reasonably be inferred from the passage?

(A) Each of the many small confrontations that occurred under the Concert of Europe threatened the integrity of the system.

(B) It provided the highest level of security possible for Europe in the late nineteenth century.

(C) All the factors contributing to stability during the late nineteenth century continue to contribute to European security.

(D) Equilibrium in the system was maintained as members grouped together to counterbalance mutual threats.

(E) It was more stable than most multipolar systems because its smaller members reacted promptly to aggression by its larger members.

(A) **INTERPRETATION (contradiction).** In fact, the small confrontations, the author maintains, made the system more stable.

**DEGREE (modifier).** "Each" means "every" in this case; we should be suspicious of such an absolute. Even if the small conflicts did threaten the integrity of the system, could we claim that each and every one, without exception, threatened the system?

(B) **DEGREE (modifier).** "Highest level of security possible" is very absolute and very difficult to justify or support.

(C) **INTERPRETATION (contradiction).** The Concert of Europe and current European systems are presented in *contrast* to each other. The current European system is unstable.

**DEGREE (modifier).** Putting the interpretation issue aside, the word "all" is very difficult to support.

(D) **CORRECT (inference).** The immediately preceding lines describe this as a characteristic of multipolar systems, and then the Concert of Europe is cited as an example. We can thus infer that the Concert of Europe possesses this characteristic.

(E) **SCOPE (out of scope).** "Most multipolar systems" is out of scope. We know nothing about the majority of multipolar systems, so we can't possibly make a comparison with the Concert of Europe.

8

In spite of a shared language, Latin American poetry written in Spanish differs from Spanish poetry in many respects. The Spanish of Latin American poets is more open than that of Spanish poets, more exposed
(5) to outside influences—indigenous, English, French, and other languages. While some literary critics maintain that there is as much linguistic unity in Latin American poetry as there is in Spanish poetry, they base this claim on the fact that Castilian Spanish, the
(10) official and literary version of the Spanish language based largely on the dialect originally spoken in the Castile region of Spain, was transplanted to the Americas when it was already a relatively standardized idiom. Although such unity may have characterized the
(15) earliest Latin American poetry, after centuries in the Americas the language of Lain American poetry cannot help but reveal the influences of its unique cultural history.

Latin American poetry is critical or irreverent in its
(20) attitude toward language, where that of Spanish poets is more accepting. For example, the Spanish-language incarnations of modernism and the avant-garde, two literary movements that used language in innovative and challenging ways, originated with Latin American
(25) poets. By contrast, when these movements later reached Spain, Spanish poets greeted them with reluctance. Spanish poets, even those of the modern era, seem to take their language for granted, rarely using it in radical or experimental ways.
(30) The most distinctive note in Latin American poetry is its enthusiastic response to the modern world, while Spanish poetry displays a kind of cultural conservatism—the desire to return to an ideal culture of the distant past. Because no Spanish-language
(35) culture lies in the equally distant (i.e., pre-Columbian) past of the Americas, but has instead been invented by Latin Americans day by day, Latin American poetry has no such long-standing past to romanticize. Instead, Latin American poetry often displays a curiosity about
(40) the literature of other cultures, an interest in exploring poetic structures beyond those typical of Spanish poetry. For example, the first Spanish-language haiku—a Japanese poetic form—were written by José Juan Tablada, a Mexican. Another of the Latin
(45) American poets' responses to this absence is the search for a world before recorded history—not only that of Spain or the Americas, but in some cases of the planet; the Chilean poet Pablo Neruda's work, for example, is noteworthy for its development of an ahistorical
(50) mythology for the creation of the earth. For Latin American poets there is no such thing as the pristine cultural past affirmed in the poetry of Spain: there is only the fluid interaction of all world cultures, or else the extensive time before cultures began.

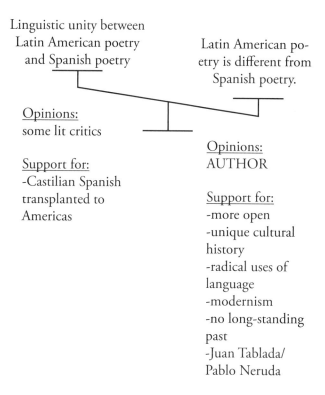

Linguistic unity between Latin American poetry and Spanish poetry

Latin American poetry is different from Spanish poetry.

Opinions: some lit critics

Support for:
-Castilian Spanish transplanted to Americas

Opinions: AUTHOR

Support for:
-more open
-unique cultural history
-radical uses of language
-modernism
-no long-standing past
-Juan Tablada/ Pablo Neruda

*Remember, don't confuse a comparison with an argument. In this case, the author certainly compares Latin American poetry with Spanish poetry, but this comparison in and of itself does not constitute an argument. The argument is that the two types of poetry are different, even though some literary critics might claim otherwise.*

8

6. The discussion in the second paragraph is intended primarily to

(A) argue that Latin American poets originated modernism and the avant-garde

(B) explain how Spanish poetry and Latin American poetry differ in their attitudes toward the Spanish language

(C) demonstrate why Latin American poetry is not well received in Spain

(D) show that the Castilian Spanish employed in Spanish poetry has remained relatively unchanged by the advent of modernism and the avant-garde

(E) illustrate the extent to which Spanish poetry romanticizes Spanish-language culture.

(A) **INTERPRETATION (unsupported).** While modernism and the avant-garde are mentioned, the author does not claim that L.A. poets *invented* modernism and the avant-garde.

(B) **CORRECT (inference).** Each paragraph is about differences between the two, and the second paragraph in particular is about the differences in attitudes about language. This is a correct interpretation for how this paragraph fits into the passage as a whole.

(C) **SCOPE (out of scope).** The way that Latin American poetry is received in Spain is not relevant or within the scope of this passage.

(D) **SCOPE (narrow).** This is in the paragraph, but this answer doesn't mention Latin American poetry.

(E) **SCOPE (out of scope).** While the Spanish poets' romanticization of past Spanish culture is within the scope of the passage, it is discussed in the third paragraph, not the second. This discussion is out of the scope of the second paragraph.

7. Given the information in the passage, which one of the following is most analogous to the evolution of Latin American poetry?

(A) A family moves its restaurant to a new town and incorporates local ingredients into its traditional recipes.

(B) A family moves its business to a new town after the business fails in its original location.

(C) A family with a two-hundred-year-old house labors industriously in order to restore the house to its original appearance.

(D) A family does research into its ancestry in order to construct its family tree.

(E) A family eagerly anticipates its annual vacation but never takes photographs or purchases souvenirs to preserve its memories.

(A) **CORRECT (synthesis).** Spanish language poets moved to Latin America and incorporated the indigenous culture into their writing. This analogy shows an understanding of the passage as a whole.

(B) **INTERPRETATION (unsupported).** The poets of Latin America did not originally fail in Spain.

(C) **INTERPRETATION (unsupported).** Latin American poetry is not attempting to restore the original characteristics of Spanish poetry.

(D) **INTERPRETATION (unsupported).** Latin American poets do not attempt to research the history of Spanish poetry.

(E) **INTERPRETATION (unsupported).** Spain is in the Latin American poets' past, not future. There is nothing to parallel "annual." Furthermore, "never" doesn't match the influence of Spanish poetry on L.A. poetry.

8

8. The passage's claims about Spanish poetry would be most weakened if new evidence indicating which one of the following were discovered?

(A) Spanish linguistic constructs had greater influence on Latin American poets than had previously been thought.

(B) Castilian Spanish was still evolving linguistically at the time of the inception of Latin American poetry.

(C) Spanish poets originated an influential literary movement that used language in radical ways.

(D) Castilian Spanish was influenced during its evolution by other Spanish dialects.

(E) Spanish poets rejected the English and French incarnations of modernism.

(A) **DEGREE (opinion).** The degree of this influence is not important. The author doesn't claim that original linguistic constructs didn't have an influence, just that there are also other influences involved.

(B) **INTERPRETATION (unsupported).** Even if the language was still evolving, this wouldn't affect the main argument, which is that Latin American poetry diverged from Spanish poetry.

(C) **CORRECT (inference).** Since the author argues that Spanish poets have been reluctant to adopt change, we can infer that such a radical movement would hurt the author's argument.

(D) **SCOPE (out of scope).** This passage is about the evolution of Spanish-language *poetry*, not the evolution of the Spanish language itself.

(E) **INTERPRETATION (contradiction).** The author argues that Spanish poets have been closed to outside influences. This answer doesn't weaken the argument. Rather, it would strengthen it!

9. The passage affirms each of the following EXCEPT:

(A) The first haiku in the Spanish language were written by a Latin American poet.

(B) Spanish poetry is rarely innovative or experimental in its use of language.

(C) Spanish poetry rarely incorporates poetic traditions from other cultures.

(D) Latin American poetry tends to take the Spanish language for granted.

(E) Latin American poetry incorporates aspects of various other languages.

(A) **IDENTIFICATION.** This is mentioned in the passage in lines 42–44.

(B) **IDENTIFICATION.** This is mentioned in the passage in lines 27–29.

(C) **IDENTIFICATION.** This is mentioned in the passage in lines 32–34.

(D) **CORRECT (contradiction).** This is the exact opposite of what is mentioned in the passage, and is therefore not affirmed.

(E) **IDENTIFICATION.** This is mentioned in the passage, in lines 38–44.

8

10. Which one of the following can most reasonably be inferred from the passage about Latin American poetry's use of poetic structures from other world cultures?

(A) The use of poetic structures from other world cultures is an attempt by Latin American poets to create a cultural past.

(B) The use of poetic structures from other world cultures by Latin American poets is a response to their lack of a long-standing Spanish-language cultural past in the Americas.

(C) The use of poetic structures from other world cultures has led Latin American poets to reconsider their lack of a long-standing Spanish-language cultural past in the Americas.

(D) Latin American poets who write about a world before recorded history do not use poetic structures from other world cultures.

(E) Latin American poetry does not borrow poetic structures from other world cultures whose literature exhibits cultural conservatism.

(A) **INTERPRETATION (unsupported).** While a relative lack of cultural history is mentioned, the author does not claim that Latin American poets are trying to *create* a cultural *past*. Rather, they are "inventing" a current culture "day by day."

(B) **CORRECT (inference).** This inference is directly supported by lines 34–42.

(C) **INTERPRETATION (unsupported).** This answer reverses the logic. It is the lack of a cultural past that causes Latin American poets to embrace other world cultures, not the other way around.

(D) **INTERPRETATION (unsupported).** While a world before recorded history is mentioned, and other world cultures are mentioned, the passage does not mention whether poets who write about prehistory use poetic structures from other cultures.

(E) **INTERPRETATION (unsupported).** It might be tempting to take Latin American poetry's divergence from a more conservative Spanish poetry as an indication of a broader

trend away from the influence of conservative cultures. However, the criteria for how Latin American poets choose their influences are not discussed. Thus, we can't make this inference without taking a big leap in reasoning.

11. Based on the passage, the author most likely holds which one of the following views toward Spanish poetry's relationship to the Spanish cultural past?

(A) This relationship has inspired Spanish poets to examine their cultural past with a critical eye.

(B) This relationship forces Spanish poets to write about subjects with which they feel little natural affinity.

(C) This relationship is itself the central theme of much Spanish poetry.

(D) This relationship infuses Spanish poetry with a romanticism that is reluctant to embrace the modern era.

(E) This relationship results in poems that are of little interest to contemporary Spanish readers.

(A) **INTERPRETATION (contradiction).** The author states that Spanish poets do the opposite—they are more "accepting" or uncritical.

(B) **SCOPE (out of scope).** The affinity of Spanish poets towards their subjects is not discussed.

(C) **INTERPRETATION (unsupported).** This is subtle. Though Spanish poetry often deals with the past, it doesn't necessarily deal with the *relationship between poetry* and the past.

(D) **CORRECT (inference).** Paragraph 3 is, in large part, about this romanticism, and the reluctance of Spanish poetry to embrace modernism.

(E) **SCOPE (out of scope).** The interests of contemporary Spanish readers are not within the scope of this passage.

**8**

12. Which one of the following inferences is most supported by the passage?

(A) A tradition of cultural conservatism has allowed the Spanish language to evolve into a stable, reliable form of expression.

(B) It was only recently that Latin American poetry began to incorporate elements of other languages.

(C) The cultural conservatism of Spanish poetry is exemplified by the uncritical attitude of Spanish poets toward the Spanish language.

(D) Latin American poets' interest in other world cultures is illustrated by their use of Japanese words and phrases.

(E) Spanish poetry is receptive to the influence of some Spanish-language poets outside of Spain.

(A) **INTERPRETATION (unsupported).** The author does not make a connection between cultural conservatism and linguistic stability.

(B) **INTERPRETATION (unsupported).** The author does not claim that this influence is a recent phenomenon.

(C) **CORRECT (inference).** The uncritical attitude of Spanish poets towards the language is mentioned as one example of the cultural conservatism of Spanish poetry (paragraph 2).

(D) **SCOPE (out of scope).** There is mention of style, but there is no mention of L.A. poets incorporating Japanese *words* and *phrases*.

(E) **INTERPRETATION (unsupported).** This statement might be true, but there is nothing in the passage that would support this interpretation.

8

According the the theory of gravitation, every particle of matter in the universe attracts every other particle with a force that increases as either the mass of the particle increase, or their proximity to one
(5) another increases, or both. Gravitation is believed to shape the structures of stars, galaxies, and the entire universe. But for decades cosmologists (scientists who study the universe) have attempted to account for the finding that at least 90 percent of the universe seems to
(10) be missing: that the total amount of observable matter—stars,dust, and miscellaneous debris—does not contain enough mass to explain why the universe is organized in the shape of galaxies and clusters of galaxies. To account for this discrepancy, cosmologists
(15) hypothesize that something else, which they call "dark matter," provides the gravitational force necessary to make the huge structures cohere.

What is dark matter? Numerous exotic entities have been postulated, but among the more attractive
(20) candidates—because they are known actually to exist—are neutrinos, elementary particles created as a by-product of nuclear fusion, radioactive decay, or catastrophic collisions between other particles. Neutrinos, which come in three types, are by far the
(25) most numerous kind of particle in the universe; however, they have long been assumed to have no mass. If so, that would disqualify them as dark matter. Without mass, matter cannot exert gravitational force; without such force, it cannot induce other matter to
(30) cohere.

But new evidence suggests that a neutrino does have mass. This evidence came by way of research findings supporting the existence of a long-theorized but never observed phenomenon called oscillation,
(35) whereby each of the three neutrino types can change into one of the others as it travels through space. Researchers held that the transformation is possible only if neutrinos also have mass. They obtained experimental confirmation of the theory by generating
(40) one neutrino type and then finding evidence that it had oscillated into the predicted neutrino type. In the process, they were able to estimate the mass of a neutrino at from 0.5 to 5 electron volts.

While slight, even the lowest estimate would yield
(45) a lot of mass given that neutrinos are so numerous, especially considering that neutrinos were previously assumed to have no mass. Still, even at the highest estimate, neutrinos could only account for about 20 percent of the universe's "missing" mass.
(50) Nevertheless, that is enough to alter our picture of the universe even if it does not account for all of dark matter. In fact, some cosmologists claim that this new evidence offers the best theoretical solution yet to the dark matter problem. If the evidence holds up, these
(55) cosmologists believe, it may add to our understanding of the role elementary particles play in holding the universe together.

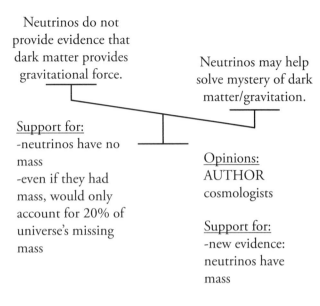

Neutrinos do not provide evidence that dark matter provides gravitational force.

Neutrinos may help solve mystery of dark matter/gravitation.

Support for:
-neutrinos have no mass
-even if they had mass, would only account for 20% of universe's missing mass

Opinions:
AUTHOR
cosmologists

Support for:
-new evidence: neutrinos have mass

*This is a challenging passage that ultimately describes the potential role neutrinos play in explaining what dark matter is, and therefore how it might affect gravitational force. For passages containing challenging subject matter and terminology, such as this one, it is especially useful to organize the information relative to how it impacts an argument.*

**8**

13. Which one of the following most accurately expresses the main idea of the passage?

(A) Although cosmologists believe that the universe is shaped by gravitation, the total amount of observable matter in the universe is greatly insufficient to account for the gravitation that would be required to cause the universe to be organized into galaxies.

(B) Given their inability to account for more than 20 percent of the universe's "missing" mass, scientists are beginning to speculate that our current understanding of gravity is significantly mistaken.

(C) Indirect evidence suggesting that neutrinos have mass may allow neutrinos to account for up to 20 percent of dark matter, a finding that could someday be extended to a complete solution of the dark matter problem.

(D) After much speculation, researchers have discovered that neutrinos oscillate from one type into another as they travel through space, a phenomenon that proves that neutrinos have mass.

(E) Although it has been established that neutrinos have mass, such mass does not support the speculation of cosmologists that neutrinos constitute a portion of the universe's "missing" mass.

(A) **SCOPE (narrow).** Though the passage does support this idea, this idea is only one part of the larger point of the passage.

(B) **INTERPRETATION (unsupported).** The author believes this research provides promise, despite its limitations, and does not hint that it shows our understanding is mistaken.

(C) **CORRECT (synthesis).** Though this is a less than ideal summary of the text, it does touch upon the central argument, and upon various other elements in the text.

(D) **SCOPE (narrow).** This is certainly mentioned in the passage, but this is merely one part in a larger picture.

(E) **INTERPRETATION (contradicted).** The fact that neutrinos have mass *is used as support* for the claim that neutrinos may constitute part of the universe's missing mass.

14. Which one of the following titles most completely and accurately expresses the contents of the passage?

(A) "The Existence of Dark Matter: Arguments For and Against"

(B) "Neutrinos and the Dark Matter Problem: A Partial Solution?"

(C) "Too Little, Too Late: Why Neutrinos Do Not Constitute Dark Matter"

(D) "The Role of Gravity: How Dark Matter Shapes Stars"

(E) "The Implications of Oscillation: Do Neutrinos Really Have Mass?"

(A) **INTERPRETATION (unsupported).** While this is close, the central argument is not whether dark matter exists; the central argument has to do more with whether neutrinos account for some of the universe's missing mass. Furthermore, this answer suggests that the passage is balanced, when in fact it is heavily weighted towards one side of the argument.

(B) **CORRECT (synthesis).** Notice that this answer pretty much sums up our scale image.

(C) **INTERPRETATION (contradiction).** This is the opposite of the author's argument.

(D) **SCOPE (out of scope).** This is in the same general subject area as the passage, but the passage does not specifically discuss how dark matter shapes stars.

(E) **SCOPE (narrow).** This is discussed in the passage, but it is just one part of a larger discussion.

8

15. Based on the passage, the author most likely holds which one of the following views?

(A) Observable matter constitutes at least 90 percent of the mass of the universe.

(B) Current theories are incapable of identifying the force that causes all particles in the universe to attract one another.

(C) The key to the problem of dark matter is determining the exact mass of a neutrino.

(D) It is unlikely that any force other than gravitation will be required to account for the organization of the universe into galaxies.

(E) Neutrinos probably account for most of the universe's "missing" mass.

(A) **INTERPRETATION (contradicted).** In fact, the passage states the exact opposite: that 90% of the universe's mass seems to be missing.

(B) **INTERPRETATION (contradicted).** The author directly states that gravitation is the force that causes particles to attract one another. While there may be missing mass, the force is not in question.

(C) **DEGREE (modifier).** Though finding out the exact mass of a neutrino will certainly be a key, the passage does not go as far as to say it is *the* key.

(D) **CORRECT (inference).** The passage works off the assumption that gravity is the force that organizes the universe, and works to explain the mysteries of the universe relative to what we know about gravity.

(E) **DEGREE (modifier).** Though neutrinos have some mass, and provide a partial explanation, the author does not go as far as to say they account for "most" of the missing mass. "Some" would be a more appropriate modifier.

16. As described in the last paragraph of the passage, the cosmologists' approach to solving the dark matter problem is most analogous to which one of the following?

(A) A child seeking information about how to play chess consults a family member and so learns of a book that will instruct her in the game.

(B) A child seeking to earn money by delivering papers is unable to earn enough money for a bicycle and so decides to buy a skateboard instead.

(C) A child hoping to get a dog for his birthday is initially disappointed when his parents bring home a cat but eventually learns to love the animal.

(D) A child seeking money to attend a movie is given some of the money by one of his siblings and so decides to go to each of his other siblings to ask for additional money.

(E) A child enjoys playing sports with the neighborhood children but her parents insist that she cannot participate until she has completed her household chores.

(A) **INTERPRETATION (unsupported).** The scientists are not going to a separate source to find the truth; they are looking for it by studying the universe.

(B) **INTERPRETATION (unsupported).** That neutrinos only provide 20% of mass has not forced the cosmologists to abandon their theory in favor of something else.

(C) **INTERPRETATION (unsupported).** The cosmologists are not disappointed, and again, there is no switch to another theory.

(D) **CORRECT (synthesis).** This analogy correctly synthesizes the elements of the last paragraph. Recent research on neutrinos gives some of the answer, and it helps the scientists figure out how to find out the rest.

(E) **INTERPRETATION (unsupported).** The idea of completing one thing before having the ability to start on another is not supported at all.

8

MANHATTAN
LSAT

17. The author's attitude towards oscillation can most accurately be characterized as being

(A) satisfied that it occurs and that it suggests that neutrinos have mass

(B) hopeful that it will be useful in discovering other forms of dark matter

(C) concerned that it is often misinterpreted to mean that neutrinos account for all of dark matter

(D) skeptical that it occurs until further research can be done

(E) convinced that it cannot occur outside an experimental setting

(A) **CORRECT (inference).** There is no suggestion that the author questions the existence of oscillation, and the author uses this property as proof that neutrinos have mass.

(B) **INTERPRETATION (unsupported).** The author does not connect oscillation with finding other types of dark matter.

(C) **DEGREE (modifier).** At no point does the author mention the idea that neutrinos might account for *all* dark matter.

   **DEGREE (opinion).** To say that the author is "concerned' about anything would be to overstate any opinion that the author might have displayed.

(D) **INTERPRETATION (contradicted).** The author is not *skeptical* of oscillation. Rather, the author seems satisfied that oscillation proves that neutrinos have mass.

(E) **SCOPE (out of scope).** A contrast between real and experimental settings is not made in this passage.

18. Which one of the following phrases could replace the world "cohere" at line 30 without substantively altering the author's meaning?

(A) exert gravitational force

(B) form galactic structures

(C) oscillate into another type of matter

(D) become significantly more massive

(E) fuse to produce new particles

(A) **INTERPRETATION (unsupported).** This is close, but wrong. The complete sentence states that it (dark matter) exerts gravitational force, and *therefore* causes coherence. The author does not say exerting gravitation force and causing to cohere are one and the same.

(B) **CORRECT (inference).** We can infer the meaning of "cohere" as follows: when dark matter exerts force, it causes matter to come together to form the structures of the universe.

(C) **SCOPE (out of scope).** Oscillation relates to a different part of the passage.

(D) **INTERPRETATION (unsupported).** There is no evidence to suggest that "cohere" means to become more massive.

(E) **INTERPRETATION (unsupported).** This is tempting, but "cohere" doesn't necessarily mean "fuse."

8

19. The passage states each of the following
EXCEPT:

(A) There are more neutrinos in the universe than
there are non-neutrinos.

(B) Observable matter cannot exert enough
gravitational force to account for the present
structure of the universe.

(C) Scientific experiments support the theory of
neutrino oscillation.

(D) Neutrinos likely cannot account for all of the
universe's "missing" mass.

(E) Dark matter may account for a large portion
of the universe's gravitational force.


(A) **CORRECT (unsupported).** This is not
mentioned in the passage.

(B) **IDENTIFICATION.** This is mentioned in
paragraphs one and four.

(C) **IDENTIFICATION.** This is mentioned in
the third paragraph.

(D) **IDENTIFICATION.** This is mentioned in
the final paragraph.

(E) **IDENTIFICATION.** This is mentioned in
the first paragraph.

8

Leading questions—questions worded in such a way as to suggest a particular answer—can yield unreliable testimony either by design, as when a lawyer tries to trick a witness into affirming a particular
(5) version of the evidence of a case, or by accident, when a questioner unintentionally prejudices the witness's response. For this reason, a judge can disallow such questions in the courtroom interrogation of witnesses. But their exclusion from the courtroom by no means
(10) eliminates the remote effects of earlier leading questions on eyewitness testimony. Alarmingly, the beliefs about an event that a witness brings to the courtroom may often be adulterated by the effects of leading questions that were introduced intentionally or
(15) unintentionally by lawyers, police investigators, reporters, or others with whom the witness has already interacted.

Recent studies have confirmed the ability of leading questions to alter the details of our memories
(20) and have led to a better understanding of how this process occurs and, perhaps, of the conditions that make for greater risks that an eyewitness's memories have been tainted by leading questions. These studies suggest that not all details of our experiences become
(25) clearly or stably stored in memory—only those to which we give adequate attention. Moreover, experimental evidence indicates that if subtly introduced new data involving remembered events do not actively conflict with our stored memory data, we
(30) tend to process such new data similarly whether they correspond to details as we remember them, or to gaps in those details. In the former case, we often retain the new data as a reinforcement of the corresponding aspect of the memory, and in the latter case, we often
(35) retain them as a construction to fill the corresponding gap. An eyewitness who is asked, prior to courtroom testimony, "How fast was the car going when it passed the stop sign?" may respond to the query about speed without addressing the question of the stop sign. But
(40) the "stop sign" datum has now been introduced, and when later recalled, perhaps during courtroom testimony, it may be processed as belonging to the original memory even if the witness actually saw no stop sign.
(45) The farther removed from the event, the greater the chance of a vague or incomplete recollection and the greater the likelihood of newly suggested information blending with original memories. Since we can be more easily misled with respect to fainter and more
(50) uncertain memories, tangential details are more apt to become constructed out of subsequently introduced information than are more central details. But what is tangential to a witness's original experience of an event may nevertheless be crucial to the courtroom issues
(55) that the witness's memories are supposed to resolve. For example, a perpetrator's shirt color or hairstyle might be tangential to one's shocked observance of an armed robbery, but later those factors might be crucial to establishing the identity of the perpetrator.

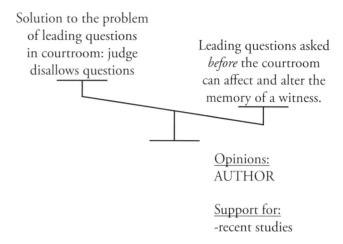

Solution to the problem of leading questions in courtroom: judge disallows questions

Leading questions asked *before* the courtroom can affect and alter the memory of a witness.

Opinions:
AUTHOR

Support for:
-recent studies

*This is a one-sided argument. The bulk of the passage discusses experimental evidence in support of the right side of the scale.*

8

20. Which one of the following most accurately expresses the main point of the passage?

(A) The unreliability of memories about incidental aspects of observed events makes eyewitness testimony especially questionable in cases in which the witness was not directly involved.

(B) Because of the nature of human memory storage and retrieval, the courtroom testimony of eyewitnesses may contain crucial inaccuracies due to leading questions asked prior to the courtroom appearance.

(C) Researchers are surprised to find that courtroom testimony is often dependent on suggestion to fill gaps left by insufficient attention to detail at the time that the incident in question occurred.

(D) Although judges can disallow leading questions from the courtroom, it is virtually impossible to prevent them from being used elsewhere, to the detriment of many cases.

(E) Stricter regulation should be placed on lawyers whose leading questions can corrupt witnesses' testimony by introducing inaccurate data prior to the witnesses' appearance in the courtroom.

(A) **SCOPE (out of scope).** The level of involvement of the witness is not a factor discussed in the passage.

(B) **CORRECT (synthesis).** This answer provides a succinct summary of the passage. Note that it matches our understanding of the central argument.

(C) **INTERPRETATION (unsupported).** While the author uses the word "alarming" to describe the effects of leading questions, we haven't been told that the researchers were "surprised."
**INTERPRETATION (unsupported).** The author does not state that witnesses pay "insufficient attention," but rather that certain details may have been tangential.
**SCOPE (narrow).** The "filling of gaps" in memory is certainly mentioned in the passage, but it's only mentioned as one research finding, not as the main point of the passage.

(D) **SCOPE (out of scope).** While the prevention of the use of leading questions in the courtroom is discussed, prevention elsewhere is not within the scope of this passage.

(E) **SCOPE (out of scope).** Though the author may agree with this opinion, it is not the central argument that is presented in the passage.

21. It can be reasonably inferred from the passage that which of the following, if it were effectively implemented, would most increase the justice system's ability to prevent leading questions from causing mistaken court decisions?

(A) a policy ensuring that witnesses have extra time to answer questions concerning details that are tangential to their original experiences of events

(B) thorough revision of the criteria for determining which kinds of interrogation may be disallowed in courtroom testimony under the category of "leading questions"

(C) increased attention to the nuances of all witnesses' responses to courtroom questions, even those that are not leading questions

(D) extensive interviewing of witnesses by all lawyers for both sides of a case prior to those witnesses' courtroom appearance

(E) availability of accurate transcripts of all interrogations of witnesses that occurred prior to those witnesses' appearance in court

(A) **SCOPE (out of scope).** Time given to answer questions is not discussed as an element that affects accuracy of memory.

(B) **INTERPRETATION (unsupported).** While leading questions in the courtroom are discussed, the main thrust of the passage deals with leading questions *before* the courtroom.

(C) **INTERPRETATION (unsupported).** While leading questions in the courtroom are discussed, the main thrust of the passage deals with leading questions *before* the courtroom.

(D) **INTERPRETATION (contradiction).** If anything, extensive interviewing by the lawyers would probably make the testimony more inaccurate, because the lawyers would have more of a chance to introduce leading questions.

(E) **CORRECT (inference).** Though this is not a great answer, the availability of accurate transcripts would allow lawyers and judges to evaluate better whether leading questions were asked, and whether these questions affected the memory of a witness.

22. Which one of the following is mentioned in the passage as a way in which new data suggested to a witness by a leading question are sometimes processed?

(A) They are integrated with current memories as support for those memories.

(B) They are stored tentatively as conjectural data that fade with time.

(C) They stay more vivid in memory than do previously stored memory data.

(D) They are reinterpreted so as to be compatible with the details already stored in memory.

(E) They are retained in memory even when they conflict with previously stored memory data.

(A) **CORRECT (identification).** This process is discussed in the second paragraph (lines 26–32).

(B) **INTERPRETATION (unsupported).** There is no evidence to suggest that the data is "tentative," "conjectural," or that it "fades with time."

(C) **DEGREE (modifier).** The new data is stored like previous memories; the author does not go as far as to say they become "more" vivid.

(D) **INTERPRETATION (unsupported).** While the new data does become compatible with details already stored in memory, the author does not say that the new data is "reinterpreted."

(E) **INTERPRETATION (contradiction).** In fact, the passage says the opposite, that the new data will be stored if it *doesn't* conflict with previously stored memory.

23. In discussing the tangential details of events, the passage contrasts their original significance to witnesses with their possible significance in the courtroom (lines 52–59). That contrast is most closely analogous to which one of the following?

(A) For purposes of flavor and preservation, salt and vinegar are important additions to cucumbers during the process of pickling, but these purposes could be attained by adding other ingredients instead.

(B) For the purpose of adding a mild stimulant effect, caffeine is included in some types of carbonated drinks, but for the purposes of appealing to health-conscious consumers, some types of carbonated drinks are advertised as being caffeine-free.

(C) For purposes of flavor and tenderness, the skins of apples and some other fruits are removed during preparation for drying, but grape skins are an essential part of raisins, and thus grape skins are not removed.

(D) For purposes of flavor and appearance, wheat germ is not needed in flour and is usually removed during milling, but for purposes of nutrition, the germ is an important part of the grain.

(E) For purposes of texture and appearance, some fat ma be removed from meat when it is ground into sausage, but the removal of fat is also important for purposes of health.

(A) **INTERPRETATION (unsupported).** There is no mention in the passage of substituting one element for another to attain a similar result.

(B) **INTERPRETATION (unsupported).** This answer describes two different, separate situations—drinks with caffeine and drinks without. There is no analogous situation in our passage.

(C) **INTERPRETATION (unsupported).** This answer is about removing something in some situations and not in others. This does not match the passage.

(D) **CORRECT (inference).** Wheat germ is not important for one part, but important for another. That parallels the lack of importance of tangential details to the witness, but an importance of these details during the trial (lines 52–55).

8

(E) **INTERPRETATION (unsupported):** This answer gives two different situations for which something is important. In the passage, tangential details are important for the trial but NOT for the witness. This doesn't match.

24. Which one of the following questions is most directly answered by information in the passage?

(A) In witnessing what types of crimes are people especially likely to pay close attention to circumstantial details?

(B) Which aspects of courtroom interrogation cause witnesses to be especially reluctant to testify in extensive detail?

(C) Can the stress of having to testify in a courtroom situation affect the accuracy of memory storage and retrieval?

(D) Do different people tend to possess different capacities for remembering details correctly?

(E) When is it more likely that a detail of an observed event will be accurately remembered?

(A) **SCOPE (out of scope).** "Types of crimes" are not discussed.

(B) **SCOPE (out of scope).** Courtroom testimony and witness reluctance are not discussed.

(C) **SCOPE (out of scope).** The stress of testifying in court is not discussed in the passage.

(D) **SCOPE (out of scope).** The differing capacities of different people are not discussed.

(E) **CORRECT (identification).** The passage states that details are more accurately remembered if they are not tangential, and if the event is closer in time to the present (lines 45–52).

25. The second paragraph consists primarily of material that

(A) corroborates and adds detail to a claim made in the first paragraph

(B) provides examples illustrating the applications of a theory discussed in the first paragraph

(C) forms an argument in support of a proposal that is made in the final paragraph

(D) anticipates and provides grounds for the rejection of a theory alluded to by the author in the final paragraph

(E) explains how newly obtained data favor one of two traditional theories mentioned elsewhere in the second paragraph

(A) **CORRECT (synthesis).** The second paragraph provides evidence that supports the argument made at the end of the first paragraph.

(B) **INTERPRETATION (unsupported).** The second paragraph is not about *applying* the argument made in the first.

(C) **INTERPRETATION (unsupported).** The second paragraph is supporting evidence, not an argument. Furthermore, there is no proposal made in the final paragraph.

(D) **INTERPRETATION (unsupported).** There is no theory mentioned in the final paragraph that this evidence helps to reject.

(E) **INTERPRETATION (unsupported).** "Two traditional theories" are not mentioned in the second paragraph.

26. It can be most reasonably inferred from the passage that the author holds that the recent studies discussed in the passage

(A) have produced some unexpected findings regarding the extent of human reliance on external verification of memory details

(B) shed new light on a longstanding procedural controversy in the law

(C) may be of theoretical interest despite their tentative nature and inconclusive findings

(D) provide insights into the origins of several disparate types of logically fallacious reasoning

(E) should be of more than abstract academic interest to the legal profession

(A) **DEGREE (opinion).** While we know that the author is "alarmed" with the findings, we don't know that the author feels these findings are unexpected.
   **INTERPRETATION (unsupported).** The passage discusses external elements (leading questions) that *affect* one's memory, but not external elements used to *verify* one's memory.

(B) **INTERPRETATION (unsupported).** "Controversy" is an incorrect interpretation of the discussion. The passage discusses findings that support a claim, but there is no controversy introduced.
   **DEGREE (modifier).** Even if we could call this a controversy, there is no evidence to suggest that "longstanding" is an accurate way to describe the situation.

(C) **INTERPRETATION (contradiction).** The author does not say the findings are tentative or inconclusive. In fact, the author states that recent studies have "confirmed" (line 18).

(D) **SCOPE (out of scope).** Inaccurate memory is discussed, but incorrect reasoning is not.

(E) **CORRECT (inference).** It is clear that the author feels that this is an important issue for the legal profession. We get a sense for the author's dismay regarding the adulteration of witness recollections in lines 12–17.

27. Which one of the following can be most reasonably inferred from the information in the passage?

(A) The tendency of leading questions to cause unreliable courtroom testimony has no correlation with the extent to which witnesses are emotionally affected by the events that they have observed.

(B) Leading questions asked in the process of a courtroom examination of a witness are more likely to cause inaccurate testimony than are leading questions asked outside the courtroom.

(C) The memory processes by which newly introduced data tend to reinforce accurately remembered details of events are not relevant to explaining the effects of leading questions.

(D) The risk of testimony being inaccurate due to certain other factors tends to increase as an eyewitness's susceptibility to giving inaccurate testimony due to the effects of leading questions increases.

(E) The traditional grounds on which leading questions can be excluded from courtroom interrogation of witnesses have been called into question by the findings of recent studies.

(A) **SCOPE (out of scope).** The emotional states of witnesses are outside the scope of this passage. They are never discussed.

(B) **DEGREE (modifier).** We have no evidence that one is any "more likely" than the other. This comparison is not made in the passage.

(C) **INTERPRETATION (contradiction).** In fact, the passage states the exact opposite in lines 26–32.

(D) **CORRECT (inference).** Though phrased in a complicated way, it essentially states that the risk of inaccurate testimony is greater when witnesses are more susceptible to giving inaccurate testimony.

(E) **INTERPRETATION (unsupported).** The passage does start off by discussing leading questions in the courtroom and judges' power to disallow these questions. Furthermore, the passage does discuss new evidence. However, this evidence is meant to support the claim that leading questions *outside* the courtroom can affect a witness's memory.

8

# ALL TEST PREP IS NOT THE SAME